THE BLOOD COVENANT

THE
BLOOD
COVENANT

the story of God's extraordinary love for you

JAMES L. GARLOW AND ROB PRICE

BEACON HILL PRESS
OF KANSAS CITY

Printed in the
United States of America

Originally published as *The Covenant* and later as
The Covenant: A Study of God's Extraordinary Love for You

Cover Design: Ryan Deo
Interior Design: Sharon Page

Library of Congress Control Number: 2013947522

10 9 8 7 6 5 4 3 2 1

From Jim Garlow:
This book is lovingly dedicated to the one who has so graciously and unselfishly shared the marriage covenant with me from January 30, 1971, until I placed her in the arms of God on April 21, 2013, at 12:50 p.m. —my wife, friend, lover, confidante, and covenant partner—Carol.

From Rob Price:
This book is dedicated to Sharon, my covenant partner in marriage, who has demonstrated unfailing love to me since our wedding day on August 3, 1991. Without her quiet wisdom and constant encouragement my contributions to this book would have remained just a dream.

JAMES L. GARLOW is an author, communicator, commentator, historian, cultural observer, and senior pastor of Skyline Wesleyan Church in San Diego. He is heard daily on over eight hundred radio outlets nationwide in his one-minute historical commentary called *The Garlow Perspective*. Jim has appeared on numerous national TV shows on NBC, ABC, CNN, Fox, MSNBC, CNBC, and Comedy Central.

Garlow has done over one thousand radio, TV, and print interviews—national and local—covering a wide range of topics: historical and theological subjects, political matters, religious liberty, marriage and family issues, and cultural trends.

In 2010, Garlow—while continuing as a San Diego pastor—was appointed by former Speaker of the House Newt Gingrich to be the chairman of ReAL (Renewing American Leadership), based in DC, along with a sister organization ReAL Action.

During California's Proposition 8 (defense of marriage) battle, he founded and led the California Pastors Rapid Response Team, a group of networked pastors committed to the sacredness of life and the sanctity of marriage.

Since 2011, Garlow has served as the national chairman of Pulpit Initiative, which spearheads the yearly Pulpit Freedom Sunday—a movement involving pastors across America—in conjunction with the Alliance Defending Freedom, an alliance of 2,200 attorneys focused on religious freedom issues.

He graduated from Drew University (PhD in historical theology), Princeton Theological Seminary (Master of Theology), Asbury Theological Seminary (MDiv), Southern Nazarene University (BA and MA), and Oklahoma Wesleyan University (AA).

His coauthored the book *Cracking Da Vinci's Code*, which made the New York Times Best Sellers list. A related book, *The Da Vinci CodeBreaker*, a dictionary with over five hundred key Da Vinci Code related terms, went on to become a best seller. *The Secret Revealed*, an expose on the New Age *The Secret*, was released in July 2007.

He coauthored *Heaven and the Afterlife* in 2009, which was followed by the 2010 release of *Encountering Heaven and the Afterlife* and in 2011, *Miracles Are for Real*, and then in 2012, *Real Life Real Miracles*, all four published by Bethany House, The Baker Group.

Other books include *How God Saved Civilization* (rereleased as *God and His People*), *A Christian's Response to Islam, The Covenant, Partners in Ministry, The 21 Irrefutable Laws of Leadership Tested by Time*, and *God Still Heals*. Jim's books have been translated into nearly a dozen languages.

Jim's wife, Carol, is a graduate of Westminster Choir College in Princeton, New Jersey. She serves as minister of prayer and intercession at Skyline Wesleyan Church. Jim and Carol have four children and five grandsons.

For more information, see www.jimgarlow.com.

ROB PRICE serves as a faculty member in the Communication Arts Department at Southwestern Assemblies of God University (SAGU) in Waxahachie, Texas. He teaches various digital media courses in TV/film. Under his leadership as executive producer, student films at SAGU have won numerous awards at film festivals around the nation.

He has also worked in pastoral ministry at Lakeview Church in Indianapolis, where he served as evangelism outreach and media outreach pastor for seven years from 1999 to 2006.

He also traveled around the world as a television reporter/producer for the Christian Broadcasting Network (CBN). His educational degrees include a bachelor's degree in broadcasting/journalism from Evangel University in Springfield, Missouri, and a master's degree in TV/film from Regent University in Virginia Beach, Virginia. He serves on the faculty council for the iNRB (Intercollegiate National Religious Broadcasters).

He has written several film screenplays and authored the historical novel *Blood Brother* in 2010, based on the biblical characters David, Jonathan, and Mephibosheth.

Rob's wife, Sharon, has a doctorate in business administration from Anderson University in Anderson, Indiana, and is also a certified public accountant (CPA) in Texas. She is a faculty member at SAGU in the Business Department.

Rob and Sharon have four children. They reside in Midlothian, Texas.

OLIVIA TAYLOR of Audrant Studios in San Diego produced the illustrations and artwork.

CONTENTS

ACKNOWLEDGMENTS

From Jim Garlow:

My sincere thanks to the following individuals:

My father, Burtis Garlow (1915-98), who by both word and example "lived the covenant" and who encouraged me to write.

My mother, Winifred Garlow, who also "lived the covenant" and who painstakingly typed my dictations and illegible scribbles for the first edition of this book in 1999.

I express heartfelt thanks also to the following persons, who each taught me a "piece" of the covenant:

Milton Green of In the Word Ministries, who called himself "a Southern Baptist carpet cleaner from Cleveland, Tennessee" and came to Dallas and touched us all.

Mike Haley, who wrote an article on the covenant for *Fulness* magazine while pastoring a Baptist church in Oklahoma.

Paul Billheimer, who wrote *Destined for the Throne*, one of the most provocative books I've ever read.

Charles Capps, a cotton farmer from the town of England, Arkansas, who taught me about our authority in Christ.

Kent Anderson, who in one sentence triggered my understanding of the major step in the covenant-making ceremony.

Henry Poteet, who in his late eighties has superb scriptural recall and is always willing to have another theological discussion about the covenant.

Malcolm Shelton, my professor at Southern Nazarene University who, even though I didn't understand it at the time, kept emphasizing that spectacular concept called "the covenant."

John Oswalt, my professor at Asbury Theological Seminary, who infected me with a passion for the Old Testament.

Lefferts Loetscher, my professor at Princeton Theological Seminary, who created in me an awareness of covenant theology.

Rob Price, who, after reading my first book on the covenant, contacted me and became my good friend and a fellow student of the concept of covenant. We had many invigorating and revelatory discussions on the topic of this book. He is a total delight with whom to work. It is an honor to coauthor this new, improved, and considerably expanded book on the covenant.

From Rob Price:

My genuine appreciation goes to the following people:

Ray Schulz, my uncle who led me in a simple prayer to accept Jesus as Lord when I was six years old and has been the spiritual mentor I can talk to day or night about God and his Word.

Malcolm Smith, a faithful expositor and compelling storyteller of God's Word for more than fifty years, whose teachings via tape, radio, and books served as the doorway to my personal revelation of covenant.

Ron Bontrager, my senior pastor at Lakeview Church in Indianapolis for seven enriching years, who often entrusted me with his pulpit and gave me the first opportunity to publicly teach and preach on covenant.

And finally, Jim Garlow, coauthor of this book and pastor at Skyline Wesleyan Church in San Diego. I am forever grateful to Jim, who shares my covenant passion and responded to my long-shot email request to discuss covenant with a complete stranger on February 16, 2007, which over time has developed into genuine friendship and directly led to the publication of this book.

SECTION I
WHY SHOULD I CARE ABOUT THE COVENANT?

1

OUR JOURNEYS INTO THE WORLD OF COVENANT

Jim's Journey

"Life changing" is a very strong term. We pastors are inclined to use it too often, such as when we sometimes promise that hearing a special speaker will be a life-changing experience. But this isn't always the case; not everything that is reported to be life changing really is.

However, the story of the covenant is an exception. Here I use the term "life changing" carefully and guardedly, for what you will read concerning the covenant will alter your thinking and significantly alter your life.

Learning about the Covenant (Jim)

It was a cold December day in Dallas in 1983 when I made my way across the city to a hotel in the northern section of town. I had no reason to suspect that my life was about to be changed. The speaker for this three-day seminar was a man named Milton Green, who came with rather unusual credentials. He liked to refer to himself as "a Southern Baptist carpet cleaner from Cleveland, Tennessee." He opened the seminar by talking about the covenant.

I had heard the word "covenant" before. I remember Professor Malcolm Shelton talking about it when I was a graduate student at Southern Nazarene University in Bethany, Oklahoma. I recall hearing John Oswalt refer to it frequently when I was in the master of divinity program at Asbury Theological Seminary in Wilmore, Kentucky. I recall Lefferts Loetscher from Princeton Theological Seminary in New Jersey referring to covenant theology in early America. All of them were superb teachers, but apparently I was not a very attentive student. Somehow I never quite grasped the teaching on covenant.

But this day would be different. Milton Green began to describe the steps of the covenant-making ceremony. He spent only a short time on it, perhaps twenty or thirty minutes, but it launched me on a pursuit that has lasted for years. As he started through the steps, it was as if scales fell off my eyes. I turned to my pastor friend Travis, who was sitting beside me, and asked, "Have you ever heard this before?" He said he had not. When Milton began referring to the new covenant, my heart was pounding in anticipation. This was truly something new.

As a result, I began to study the covenant with intensity. I searched the Scriptures over and over—and for the first time in my life I wore the cover right off my Bible. Over the course of the next decade I would have numerous dialogues with my friend Pastor Henry Poteet, asking him repeatedly what he knew about this concept called the covenant. I preached on that topic in city after city, and each time I saw lives changed. It was the first time I had ever witnessed such a dramatic change of that sort. The covenant was impacting others the same way it had me.

The Covenant Is Foundational (Jim)

So why was this happening? What is it about the covenant that is so life changing? From my studies I discovered some remarkable insights. For one thing, understanding the steps of the covenant-making ceremony and its role in human history causes many

Bible verses to spring to life with meanings that may not have been previously considered.

Looking closer, I found that in many ways the covenant is the foundation of our faith and the epicenter of what we understand about our relationship with God. Upon it is based our understanding of salvation, holiness, healing, worship, deliverance, and sanctification. The covenant is truly foundational, and discovering this can be exhilarating—even life changing. Through the contents of this book, you will gain a sound understanding of the covenant and its significance.

It could be said that the entire Bible is organized around six covenants. Think of it. All of Scripture could be understood if we would simply mentally view the Bible as being constructed around six different "contracts" God made with humanity. (We will later discover that instead of six, there were actually only four. But we'll talk more about that later.)

Rob's Journey

Ever discover something new that you later realized you should've known a long time ago? Like the fact raisins really do taste better with chocolate? Or that yogurt goes from bland to bliss when you mix in granola? Stumbling on different snack combinations is fun, but sometimes new discoveries take on a much deeper significance.

It was the fall of 1992. I was living in Waxahachie, Texas, a small town just south of the Dallas/Fort Worth metroplex. Newly married to my wife, Sharon, and fresh off four years of college at a Christian school, I was now in the "work force" ready to launch my career in communications.

Revelation on Radio (Rob)

I had landed a poorly paying job up at a video production company on the north end of Dallas, but at least it was in my career field. The lonely drive to work was a solid fifty minutes.

That's a good chunk of God-time every day. Five days a week times one hundred minutes a day is five hundred minutes. My math says that's more than eight hours a week that I could spend either talking to God, worshipping him, or listening to good Bible teaching about him.

I did quite a bit of all three during those morning and afternoon drives. When I got to work I would often flip on the radio when possible to continue listening to God's Word being taught by some of the best teachers in the country. Other radio broadcasts featured timely commentary and interviews on important issues of the day. My lineup included David Jeremiah, Tony Evans, Marlin Maddux, and several others. All were fantastic feeders into my life.

But there was one Bible teacher who particularly caught my attention. His name was Malcolm Smith. What he was teaching would fundamentally redirect the course of my walk with God.

What I heard for the first time in my life was an amazing journey into the world of "covenant." Malcolm's insightful retelling of the covenant relationships between David and Jonathan and Mephibosheth caused the lightbulbs to begin flashing inside my head. This simple story, tucked between several passages inside 1 and 2 Samuel, proved to be the seed of spiritual transformation in my life. I remember thinking, "If this is true, this is going to have huge implications in my life."

The Why Behind the What (Rob)

I already knew from my understanding of Scripture and from the Spirit's witness that blood was required for forgiveness of sins and that Jesus was a sinless blood sacrifice. But I never knew the glorious "why" behind the "what" of the gospel and how it related to the character and purposes of God. I also had a difficult time putting the Bible's sixty-six books all together into any logical connection or deeper themes that would make them cohesive with a consistent message.

Covenant revelation was changing all that—and quickly.

My hunger for more knowledge and revelation exploded. I felt as if I was thrust into a completely new trajectory in the kingdom of God! I wanted to know all there was to know about his covenants with humankind. I wanted to understand more of God's covenant character. I wanted to see what the Bible felt like when viewed through a covenant lens. The journey of discovery during those early years was absolutely exhilarating.

It still is.

My developing covenant relationship with God and his covenant Word began to affect my prayer life. Bible readings and personal devotional time became a true joy. I prayed with more authority and with more faith. My confidence soared to come boldly before the throne of grace.

Covenant revelation found its natural way into how I could present the gospel to the lost. The good news became much more than just "God loves you and has a plan for your life." Frankly, that kind of oversimplified attempt at evangelism just wasn't enough information or inspiration to help the cynical American mind-set understand God's fantastic plan.

"Why Didn't Anybody in Church Ever Tell Me This?" (Rob)

Before 1992, I had no real clue what covenant meant besides some kind of vague agreement or promise between two people. I figured it was basically a glorified contract at best. How shallow was my thinking. So as this covenant revelation was revealed, an unfortunate road bump emerged in my spirit. I became frustrated and angry. Not at God, but at the church's failure in my own Pentecostal circles to teach what is undoubtedly the single most important topic in the Bible.

Why hadn't I ever heard this teaching before? I can't count how many sermons, Sunday school lessons, Bible studies, and college chapels I had attended up to that point in my life. Easily in the hundreds. Yet none had the impact of that one twenty-minute story that I wore out listening to over and over on cassette tape after first hearing it on radio.

Looking back now, I realize I shouldn't have assigned blame to any one particular pastor or local church. I've come to believe that a deficiency and a neglect in covenant understanding and application has been creeping into the American church for at least one hundred years. I view today's general lack of covenant preaching and teaching in America more as Satan's attempts to veil the truths of covenant revelation in order to tranquilize and declaw the power of the gospel.

I began to feel God's gentle tap on my shoulder. I was to be his mouthpiece in my generation to shout covenant from the rooftops.

I began Bible studies on covenant. I preached on it in prisons and in churches around Indiana. I wrote a novel about the David-Jonathan-Mephibosheth covenant relationship, called *Blood Brother*, and a full-length stage play on the same topic, called *What If It's True?* It was performed several times at Lakeview Church when I was a member of the pastoral team.

Covenant Makes a Comeback after Eighteen Hundred Years

On June 16-18, 1885, Professor H. Clay Trumbull was asked to give a series of lectures. He chose to lecture on a topic that would eventually find its way into a book titled *The Blood Covenant: A Primitive Rite and Its Bearings on Scripture*. So positive was the response to this book that a second edition, with much added material, was released in January 1893. The book is a classic, for it opens new ground in understanding the depth of God's covenant love for us articulated in the pages of Scripture.

Unfortunately by the early 1900s, the basic message of his book fell by the wayside, and the term "covenant" was not generally understood by most of the people who could benefit from its inexplicable privileges and promises.

In the years that would follow the second edition of Dr. Trumbull's writings, numerous writers would attempt to put it in popular form, including E. W. Kenyon's *The Blood Covenant*, released in 1969 posthumously by his daughter, Ruth Kenyon.

Since the early 1990s, the Holy Spirit has inspired more books to be written about covenant. Beside the first release of this book (originally titled *The Covenant*), other works include *The Lost Secret of the New Covenant* by Malcolm Smith, *The Blood Covenant* by Theo Wolmarans, and *Our Covenant God* by Kay Arthur. Another outstanding resource on covenant, *Christ and the Covenants* by O. Palmer Robertson, was originally published in 1981.

More teaching and preaching on covenant is making its way back to America's pulpits. John Hagee's national platform is one of them. He has publicly stated, "If I had but one sermon to preach it would be on the blood covenant."[1]

In addition to Jim and a handful of other church leaders in America, Rob also interviewed African pastor Jackson Senyonga. He spoke about the return of covenant in the national mind-set in his home country Uganda. "The president and the first lady and a few people in the parliament called the church together at the end of 1999. We went to the largest stadium in Uganda to rededicate the nation to God and to make a covenant as a nation to God to serve him for the next thousand years. We divorced witchcraft, idolatry, and bloodshed in this country. We not only declared it out loud but the president signed a document stating it."[2]

Jackson indicated that since the establishment of a national covenant to God, Uganda has become a model for other African nations because of its expansion of free enterprise, infrastructure, and factories. He also reported that the percentage of Ugandans diagnosed with the AIDS virus dropped dramatically from 33 percent to 5 percent in just five years.

The Assumption from Ancient Cultures

We return to the question of why something as important as the covenant is rarely mentioned except in casual reference. Why doesn't the Bible refer to it more and explain it better?

Dr. Trumbull in his late nineteenth-century classic work deals very well with that specific issue: "It seems strange that a primitive rite like the Blood Covenant, with its world-wide sweep, and its manifold applications to the history of sacrifice, should have received so little attention. . . . The suggestion of any real importance in the religious symbolism of this rite has been generally brushed aside without its receiving due consideration."[3]

But there is an even further explanation for why it is not thoroughly explained in the Bible itself. Simply stated:

Because the primitive rite of Blood Covenanting was *well-known* in the Lands of the Bible, at the time of the writing of the Bible, for that very reason we are not to look to the Bible for specific explanations of the rite itself, even where there are incidental references in the Bible to the rite and its observances; but, on the other hand, we are to find an explanation of the biblical illustrations of the primitive rite, in the understanding of that rite which we gain from outside sources. In this way, we are able to see in the Bible much that otherwise would be lost sight of.[4]

In other words, the Bible doesn't need to give a thorough explanation of the covenant, because the people in that time simply understood its significance and importance. They didn't even need to mention the word "covenant" at times because many other words in common vocabulary referred to covenant.

This is easily illustrated with an analogy using America's pastime. Imagine you overheard a conversation at a restaurant at the next table. You hear the terms "strike," "bat," "home run," "out," "pitch," "shortstop," "pop-up," "dugout," "foul," "single," "full count," and "infield." You would know instantly they were talking about baseball without ever actually mentioning the name of the game.

The words surrounding the term "covenant" include "love," "kindness," "mercy," "faithfulness," "friendship," and "loyalty." These words all have specific, not generic, meanings. Anyone living in ancient times when the Bible was being written would have easily identified these words as referring to a covenant relationship.

Other covenant words and phrases include "in," "with," "joined to," "together with," "oath," "swear," "treaty," "testament," "blessings," "curses," and "remember." When one understands the language of covenant words, the Bible takes its readers to an entirely new level of understanding. Covenant language will be discussed in further detail in chapter 4.

Unfortunately, twenty-first-century Westerners have a distinct disadvantage. So many of us today do not read the Bible with the same covenant "filter" as Easterners from ancient times. We don't have the same type of classical covenant-making ceremonies in our Western culture. The closest example is a typical wedding ceremony. Thus, we are limited in our ability to relate to this remarkable event and its profound implications in demonstrating the intensity of God's love and passion for us.

Login Required

Understanding the depth of covenant does not require special understanding or intellectual prowess. But the Bible does reveal one single requirement in order to begin walking in the fullness of covenant revelation.

Reverence for God.

It's something you must simply have before you begin your journey of fully knowing the spirit of what a covenant really is.

Read Psalm 25:14 in the different versions provided. Take them all in slowly to understand this critical component.

The LORD confides in those who fear him; he makes his covenant known to them. (NIV)

The secret of the LORD is with those who fear Him, and He will show them His covenant. (NKJV)

The LORD is a friend to those who fear him. He teaches them his covenant. (NLT)

The friendship of Jehovah is with them that fear him; and he will show them his covenant. (ASV)

The secret [of the sweet, satisfying companionship] of the Lord have they who fear (revere and worship) Him, and He will show them His covenant and reveal to them its [deep, inner] meaning. (AMP)

The Amplified version really nails it, suggesting there are layers and layers of covenant revelation waiting for the one who walks in holy fear of the King. Reverence for God triggers authentic friendship with God. True friendship with God reveals the covenant revelation of God.

Simply put: no reverence equals no revelation.

It is as if God's covenant heart is so sacred and sensitive that he doesn't share it with just anybody. Sounds strange, but it's true. James 4:6 even corroborates this reality: "God opposes the proud, but gives grace to the humble" (ESV). If a person's heart is set against God, he or she will never be open to God's covenant graces in the first place. There has to be a measure of honor and respect for God in order for God to open his heart to a human being.

Aren't we the same way? We don't bare our hearts and souls to just every stranger on the street. We must both earn the trust of others and give respect to others before relational bonds develop. It's how every strong marriage, which is a type of covenant, begins and continues to grow over time. The Godhead desires to be married to humankind through the Bridegroom in Jesus Christ.

After establishing a heart of deep reverence for God as our Creator, we are now candidates for the journey. And that expedition begins with properly defining exactly what a covenant is.

2

WHAT IS A COVENANT AND WHY IS IT SO IMPORTANT?

The Hebrew word for covenant is *berith* or *b'rit*, which simply means "to cut, to bind together in obligation." It is used nearly three hundred times in the Bible and comes from the root word meaning "to cut."[1] But a more expanded definition of the word "covenant" is required to gain a rich understanding.

Covenant is

- An all-encompassing agreement between two parties with clearly outlined perimeters and promises
- A mutual understanding between two persons who bind themselves together with specific obligations to fulfill
- The giving of oneself or a group of individuals into a lasting union together for life and unto death
- Entered into so as to complement strengths and weaknesses (never based on unilateral similarities)
- A tangible expression of love and trust
- A relationship that will require blood to be shed to reinforce the solemnity and seriousness of the bond

A covenant bond is very different from a contract agreement. How so? A contract is limited to the giving of goods, services, and products to another party. These terms may be negotiated or cancelled. What's more, contracts are made with ink. Covenants are made with blood and involve the giving of one's complete self to another—much more than just goods, services, or products!

The difference between a covenant and a contract cannot be overstated. Another way of looking at it might be to say that a blood covenant's obligations overwhelm the requirements of a contract, but a contract's requirements can't hold a candle to the obligations of a blood covenant.

These definitions explain why covenant is the highest and most honored expression of a relationship possible between two parties. Ancient Arabs even believed a covenant friendship supersedes a relationship between genetic family members. The common phrase used was "blood is thicker than milk." The interpretation being that two people bonded together to become brothers by a blood covenant are closer than two biological brothers bonded together by having drawn nourishment as babies from the same mother's milk.

There is no such thing as a casual covenant. Those two words "casual" and "covenant" are antithetical to each other. Covenant is ultimate commitment. Covenant is sacrificial. Covenant is selfless. The key Hebrew term that describes the working out of a covenant relationship is the word *chesed* (also spelled *hesed*). It is pronounced in Hebrew with a strong guttural vibration from the back of the mouth. It's no coincidence that even the sound of this powerful word *chesed* reverberates a type of passion when uttered.

Its translation into English in many Bible translations is "mercy," which is very unfortunate. The word "mercy" is often defined as "pity, clemency, forgiveness." That just doesn't accurately describe *chesed*, which Hebrews saw as the active pursuit of wanting to bless one's covenant partner!

Chesed involves the action steps of covenant. It is an intense type of emotion deep inside the spirit that is steeped in desire to bless the covenant partner. It is a pit bull love. It is tenacious. It is unending. *Chesed* is both the attitude and the action that cries out, "I want to do this for my covenant partner!" not "Well, I guess I'm obligated to do this for my covenant partner. Shucks." There is a huge difference between them. The former is heartfelt desire. The latter is begrudging duty.

A better English translation of *chesed* is "kindness" or "loving-kindness," and some Bibles do use these terms. But as a general rule, the loss of the real meaning of covenant word *chesed* may have contributed to the loss of covenant revelation over the centuries.

No Way Out

It must be emphasized that there is no way out of a blood covenant except by death. Once someone is in a covenant, the bumper rails of death hover on two sides. This is why covenants are signed in blood not just ink.

In ancient cultures when nations, tribes, or families would enter into covenant with another party, one of the verbal oaths exchanged often revealed these rails as they sacrificed an animal: "We will keep this blood covenant with you all even if we must die to protect it. And if we break the terms of this blood covenant may what happened to this animal happen to us."

The animal referred to here was the blood sacrifice of the covenant ceremony, which will be discussed in a later chapter. That animal was typically slaughtered by the cutting of its jugular vein and then cut in half from top to bottom near the spine. Not an honorable way to die for a human, which is why covenants were never entered into casually.

As gruesome a penalty that a breach of covenant would invoke, it must be underscored that covenants were also highly sought after because of the security, strength, and love birthed from such a powerful relationship. The heart of covenant is life giving. Remember the descriptive words that encompass the spirit of a covenant relationship: "unending love," "overflowing kindness," "tender mercy," "trusted faithfulness," "committed friendship," and "eternal loyalty."

Two Types of Covenants

Throughout the ancient Middle East during the period between 2000 BC to 1500 BC covenant making was a social norm between nations, tribes, and families. But history reveals there were actually two different types of covenants. Let's carefully examine the differences. In simplest terms a covenant was either an equal party or unequal party covenant. The equal party covenant (also called a parity covenant) typically provided a fair and equitable benefit to both parties and increased overall quality of life. It was freely entered into by both parties and made primarily to complement strengths and weaknesses.

For example, a warrior-based tribe lacking in agricultural skills might enter into covenant with an agricultural-based tribe lacking in warrior skills. The warriors agree to protect and preserve the people and lands of the agricultural tribe. In return, the agricultural tribe agrees to provide healthy food for the warrior tribe and properly harvest its conquered lands. Both parties freely enter into the covenant. Both parties benefit as weaknesses are covered by the other tribe's strengths. It is an equally and mutually beneficial covenant that brings much joy, love, friendship, and peace to both tribes.

The other type of covenant was an unequal party covenant (also called a unilateral or suzerain-vassal covenant). This version was in play when a greater nation, tribe, family, or individual conquered a lesser nation, tribe, family, or individual. Instead of utterly destroying the defeated foe, the greater party would "impose" a covenant upon the weaker party. This meant that the weaker party would be allowed to live, but with new stipulations. These new arrangements required the absolute allegiance of the lesser lord to the greater lord.

The suzerain (greater lord) could choose this option of covenant rather than a scorched earth policy for many reasons, usually involving the discretionary use of money, land, resources, and labor from the vassal (lesser lord). Despite its seemingly lopsided arrangement, the greater king put himself under serious obligations to provide security, peace, and assistance to the conquered king.

When carefully arranged, this type of covenant brought much blessing to both parties over the course of time. This is because the presence of a covenant was designed to prevent tyranny, dictatorship, and despotism.

The Bible Writers Just "Knew" Something

Beginning with the author of Genesis, traditionally Moses, and ending with John and the book of Revelation, all forty inspired writers of the Bible seemed to intuitively know the same "something." There was something Abraham knew about, that David knew about, that Paul knew about. Whether it was a psalm, a prayer, a story, a word of doctrine, the writers and Bible characters they wrote about seemed to be playing off of something, inferring something, living with unusual authority based on this same "something." This something was covenant.

In his book *The Lost Secret of the New Covenant*, Malcolm Smith offers a summary definition of covenant that captures the essence of this type of relationship: "A covenant is a binding, unbreakable obligation between two parties, based on unconditional love sealed by blood and sacred oath, that creates a relationship in which each party is bound by specific undertakings on each other's behalf. The parties to the covenant place themselves under the penalty of divine retribution should they later attempt to avoid those undertakings. It is a relationship that can only be broken by death."[2]

Why is "covenant" such a significant term? It is simply this: "covenant" is a word that describes God's relationship to you and me. Since the very creation of the world, God had used a unique pattern, a unique cultural event, referred to as the covenant. Through this he outlined specific requirements and spectacular promises and tells us how he wants us to respond to him, outlining the promises of what will happen if we follow his ways. And those promises are absolutely thrilling—and, as stated earlier, even life changing, as you will discover in the next few pages.

3

STEPS OF A COVENANT CEREMONY*

Covenants involve ceremony. Without them, these solemn agreements lack remembrance and validity. Such an important occasion simply requires certain steps and moments that forever mark the covenant process.

The same is true for how America negotiates the transition to new leadership in the White House. No one elected US president on the first Tuesday of November would just move into the Oval Office on Wednesday and start leading the country. There is a big day two months later in January when the official inauguration takes place. The nation watches as the important ceremony unfolds. One of the steps of the day even draws from a covenant-making ceremony, when the leader takes an oath of office and then calls upon assistance from heaven: ". . . so help me God."

Long before US presidents began to be inaugurated, cultures from across the world have engaged in covenant-making ceremonies to officially establish a covenantal relationship. These ceremonies included serious steps. This chapter will outline these powerful stages. It is important to note that not all of the same

---

*"Acting Out the Covenant," an engaging covenant learning activity for small groups and other gatherings, is available free online at www.BeaconHillBooks.com/go/Blood Covenant.

covenant procedures are used in every covenant ceremony across every culture throughout history. Different people groups over time have adopted unique variations of these steps or omitted some moments of the covenant-making process.

The Hittite and Babylonian cultures of the era between 2000 BC and 1500 BC in the Middle East were well known for making covenants. The Hittites descended from the children of Heth (a son of Canaan) and are listed in Genesis as one of the twelve Canaanite nations. The Babylonians are more commonly recognized as a culture predominant for centuries in Mesopotamia (present-day Iraq).

Abram was born and raised in this general culture. It was common for tribal chiefs or heads of city-states to enter into covenants or alliances with one another. So when God wanted to communicate to humanity, he used the covenant, because it was a vehicle people would immediately understand. After the fall of Adam and Eve and at the time of Abram, creation had gone awry.

Making covenant would be a way God could demonstrate his love for humanity and his deep desire to have fellowship with individuals. Entering into covenant was a language that even pagan cultures would understand. It is not by accident that the Old Testament of the Bible is called the old covenant nor that the New Testament is called the new covenant.

The covenant-making ceremony was an agreement between two people, families, tribes, or nations. It involved several steps that were completed publicly in an open field before a crowd of witnesses.[1]

Representative

Every covenant that was not between two individuals required a representative who would speak and act on behalf of the entire family, tribe, or nation. This special individual, carefully chosen by each party, had to be of the same bloodline as the rest of the party. A covenant representative could not be a hired hand or outsider. It was usually someone who already held a position of great importance and honor within the party.

It could be said that the nation was "in him" throughout the course of the covenant ceremony. In other words, each observer would be able to rightfully say, "What happens to him happens to me." This person would figuratively "embody" the heart, passion, intentions, and spirit of the people as the covenant ceremony proceeded. Once completed this individual would serve as the guarantor that the covenant promises would be kept.

Terms

Specific responsibilities would be clearly laid out in full view of each tribe. These would be details on how their covenant love would be expressed toward one another. Such promises clearly spelled out how they would give and receive blessing from each other. Examples might include military protection, business trade, agricultural harvesting, and educational expertise/knowledge. These terms or laws of the covenant were documented and written down for crystal clear remembrance. Two copies were made, one for each party.

Blood Sacrifice

Each covenant required the sacrifice of an animal or several animals. The animal must be cut.[2] Normally a heifer would be laid on its back and sliced down the underside of its belly. Its legs would then be folded out. The sacrifice of the animal is why we term this kind of covenant the *blood* covenant. The visible result is a bloody path on the ground as two pieces of torn flesh lay spread out opposite each other. This element of the sacrifice whispers back to the very meaning of the word "covenant," which means "to cut" in Hebrew. You don't "make" a covenant as much as you "cut" a covenant!

The blood symbolized an entering into a type of death to self and passing through to a new life of union together with the new covenant partner. At this point in the covenant-cutting ceremony the solemnity of the moment would be heightened for both parties.

Walk of Death

At this point in the ceremony, the covenant partners stood facing each other in an open field. The animal lay cut open between them. The partners literally walked through the mass of blood. One would walk through and come back on the left side. The other would come back through, turning toward the right. Together they patterned a figure eight that symbolized infinity.[3]

Each representative's soles, ankles, and even lower calves were now dripping in covenant sacrifice blood. Now blood is touching each representative, which means it's also symbolically touching each and every person from both parties gathered to watch the ceremony!

The Mark on the Body

Heifer blood on the representative's body is one thing, but the exposure of one's own human blood took the ceremony to an even deeper level. This was called the covenant seal or the covenant mark on the body. This most often took place somewhere on the right hand. In the Hebrew culture the hand includes what we would call the wrist. The covenant partners made an incision on their wrists, and the two would then put their wrists together, mingling their blood in what is called "the striking of hands."

Some primitive cultures still practice this, taking an abrasive substance like gunpowder and rubbing it in to darken the area under the skin and make the wound more pronounced so that there is a permanent mark on the body.[4] Some traditions say that the modern custom of waving our hand in greeting originates from the practice of raising hands in such a way to reveal the covenant mark.

By doing so, one person let another know that he or she had a covenant partner. This suggests that the origin of the handclasp, as in the shaking of hands, comes from the cutting of a covenant.[5]

The two individuals would clasp hands as the blood from their freshly cut wrists flowed together. The covenant mark on the wrists or palms might be what is referred to in Isaiah 49:16, in which God states, "I have engraved you on the palms of my hands."

British speaker/author Malcolm Smith, who has been teaching and preaching on the blood covenant since the 1960s, shares an amazing account of a covenant seal in action in a modern-day context.

I was in Kenya and went into the bank to change my dollars into Kenyan shillings. I came to the counter with my interpreter and the teller spread out all five fingers with her palm facing me. I looked at my interpreter and said, "What do I do?" And he said, "Do the same." So I put up my fingers, and our fingers touched and we did the transaction. I got my money and went out. And I said, "What on earth was happening in there?" He said, "Covenant. In this part of Kenya when we make covenant we cut the tips of our fingers and then we mingle the blood at each fingertip. Once that is done you are bound unto death to the person. When you do a business transaction as in the bank, you are saying that you are trusting the other that this shall be exactly as you say it is. So it's not blood covenant but it's covenant and people accept it as covenant."[6]

Oaths and Vows

Words are important as actions in a covenant-cutting ceremony. Representatives faced each other and spoke on behalf of the nation or tribe with a sobering affirmation. Their bloody right hands were raised. The specific words would vary among cultures, but all vocalized two important oaths: "We will keep the terms of this blood covenant with you even at the cost of my own bloodshed unto death! And if we fail to keep the terms of this covenant, may what happened to this animal happen to us!"

They called upon a third party deity to oversee the covenantal oaths, asking God (or a false god if it was a pagan covenant) for strength to keep the covenant. They also asked deity to administer either blessings or curses as appropriate: "So long as you keep the terms of this covenant, blessed shall you be when you go out and when you come in. Blessed shall you be when you rise up and when you lay down. Blessed shall be your wife, blessed shall be your children, blessed shall be all that you put your hands to."

Because the culture revolved around an agrarian or agricultural economy, the representative would say, "Blessed shall be your oxen, your donkeys, your fields, and the produce of your fields." After a pause, the representative would continue: "But if you violate the terms of this covenant, cursed shall you be when you rise up and lay down. Cursed shall be your wife, your children. Cursed shall be your oxen, your donkeys, your land." And on and on the representative would go, and at the end, the covenant partner would pronounce the same blessings and curses.

Covenant Meal

The covenant partners then sat at a table before the witnesses and shared a meal. But the partners didn't begin by feeding themselves. They fed each other the first few bites, saying, "As you are ingesting this food, you are ingesting me; you are taking me into your life." When a bride and a groom feed each other cake today, the act is symbolic of the covenant-making ceremony. The typical food was bread, symbolic of flesh. The typical drink was fruit of the vine, symbolic of blood. At the end of this ceremonial meal, the covenant was considered to be officially valid and in full effect.

The covenant meal will be explored in more detail in chapter 15.

Memorials

The two parties may decide to commemorate the covenant by means of some visible sign both for themselves and for generations to come. The location of the memorial was typically at the location of where the covenant was cut. Memorials may come in the form of a stone altar or pile of stones, planting of a tree(s), or digging of wells. God often uses a much grander scale for his people to "remember" a covenant. Noah's covenant was a rainbow. Moses' (or the Sinaitic) covenant was a pair of mountain ranges (Gerazim and Ebal).

It can even be said that there was an additional memorial for the people of Israel in the Sinaitic covenant during Joshua's leadership. This occurred when Israel crossed the Jordan River and Joshua instructed men from the twelve tribes to each take a large boulder out of the water. They set up the twelve stones as an altar in their new land, as a conversation piece for future generations. The altar was designed for young children to beg the question: "Daddy, why are these stones here?" The father would then have an opportunity for a fantastic illustrated sermon on God's covenant faithfulness to his people as they miraculously crossed the Jordan River!

Powerful Exchanges

Covenants of this time period also incorporated up to five key exchanges: robes, belts, weapons, names, and sons. These elements are placed last in this list, but the moments when these exchanges occurred during the covenant ceremony may have varied among cultures.

Exchange of Robes

Robes represented an exchange of identity. The two representatives would take their outer garments and exchange them. What does this represent? It symbolizes an exchange of identity, even an intentional "confusing of identity." If someone saw one of the partners from a distance, he or she might say, "Here comes Daniel. But wait—he doesn't walk like Daniel; he's not built like Daniel. But isn't that Daniel's robe he's wearing?"

Exchange of Belts and Weapons

Belts represented an exchange of strength. These belts were larger than we wear today and were the place from which military gear was hung. Exchanging them symbolized the sharing of strengths or assets. If we (Jim and Rob) entered into a covenant and exchanged belts, each of us would say to the other, "Everything I bring to this relationship is now yours. And everything you have is now mine. Our strengths and our assets are now combined."

Weapons hung on the belt. Their trade symbolized an exchange of enemies and declared that the covenant partners would protect each other from harm. "Your enemy is now my enemy." This is why the Israelites were forced into aiding the Gibeonites when their enemies—the five kings of the Amorites—attacked them in Joshua 10. (The Gibeonites had deceived Israel into making a covenant of peace with them, and now Joshua and his forces were obligated by covenant to fight on their behalf.) This covenant was so powerful that God even stopped the sun from moving for an entire day at Joshua's request to allow Israel to defeat the five kings under the light of day.

Exchange of Names

What someone was called after a covenant was critical. The name of a person was understood to be a window to one's true person. The partners once again stood facing each other in the open field. Let's again suppose we (Jim and Rob) were making a covenant with each other. I (Jim) would say, "Rob, in order to let my enemies know who my covenant partner is, I will take your name and put it in the middle of mine. No longer will I be known simply as Jim Garlow. From this moment I will be known as Jim *Price* Garlow." And I (Rob) would respond: "From this moment on, my name will be Rob *Garlow* Price, so that every time my name is pronounced, it tells all the people who my covenant partner is."

This name change is precisely what occurred when God made covenant with Abram. The man's name changed from Abram to

Abr*AH*am. The Hebrew letter for "H" was added to his name. This came from the central consonant of God's name Yahweh (YHWH).[7] This covenant name of God appears approximately sixty-eight hundred times in the Old Testament. God doesn't stop there. True to covenant, he takes Abraham's name. From this point on, he calls himself "the God of Abraham." More on this account in chapter 6.

Exchange of the Oldest Male Child

The ultimate exchange made was the oldest male child. Tradition stated that in order to "seal" the agreement, to prove the covenant was for real, the two covenant representatives (or partners if it was just a covenant between two individuals) would exchange oldest sons. The sons would actually move into the home of the partner to be raised. It was a painful event, but one that would prove the covenant was for real.

In the most grueling test of his lifetime, Abraham lived out this last step of the covenant partnership. Genesis 22:1-2 tells us, "God *tested* Abraham, and said to him, 'Abraham!' And he said, 'Here I am.' He said, 'Take now your son'" (NASB, emphasis added). Abraham didn't balk; he knew that exchanging sons was part of the covenant-making ceremony. If he was going to receive what God promised him, he had to give his son to God. So Isaac headed up the mountain with Abraham.

This event in Abraham's covenant with God will be further examined in chapter 6.

4

🔱

COVENANT LANGUAGE AND COMMON TERMS

As mentioned with the baseball analogy in chapter 1, covenant has its own set of special words and phrases that mark its presence and power. It is vitally important to be aware of this covenant language as one examines the Bible. Observing them with an informed "covenant filter" will cause these words to lift off the pages of Scripture with easier interpretation and application. In fact, if this filter is in operation, you will discover the hidden meaning of the covenant in a variety of words. Let's examine some of them.

Relationship Words

In terms of how the relationship can be honored, let's examine the following translations for the following covenant words:
- Kindness
- Mercy
- Peace
- Steadfast
- Faithfulness
- Loyalty
- Friendship

In an earlier chapter, the Hebrew word *chesed* was defined as the "action" of living out a covenant toward one's partner. It is a word loaded with passion and energy that refers to whatever a person is led to do out of covenant love for the partner. Unfortunately, when the Bible was translated into English there wasn't a strong enough word to accurately describe *chesed*. Translators chose the word "kindness," "loving-kindness," or "mercy." Those words are a nice attempt but don't quite hit the mark on the power of *chesed*.

The words "steadfast" and "faithfulness" speak to the ongoing and unending nature of a covenant as long as both parties are still alive. These words give confidence that one covenant partner will never leave or forsake the other covenant partner!

Lamentations 3:22-24 is absolutely loaded with covenant language: "The **steadfast** love of the LORD never ceases, his **mercies** never come to an end; they are new every morning; great is your **faithfulness**" (NRSV, emphasis added).

Two other covenant words take fidelity to an even deeper level: "loyalty" and "friendship." It is these words that strike at the true heart of an individual. It's one thing to be obligated to keep covenant by being steadfast or faithful. But loyalty is defined as the *feeling* of duty not just the act of duty. True friendship reveals deep trust, sharing of secrets and even tender vulnerability. On the last night of Jesus' earthly life he told his disciples, "I no longer call you servants, because a servant does not know his master's business. Instead, I have called you friends, for everything that I learned from my Father I have made known to you" (John 15:15). This is covenant talk.

Identification Words

In terms of identifying a covenant partner, look for these covenant phrases and prepositions:
- In
- With

- Together with
- Joined to
- Included in

One of the most packed sequences of this type of covenant language is found in Ephesians 2:4-10. Paul was a covenant-minded man, always reminding his readers about their covenant with God through Jesus Christ.

> But because of his great love for us, God, who is rich *in mercy*, made us alive *with* Christ even when we were dead in transgressions—it is by grace you have been saved. And God raised us up *with* Christ and seated us *with him* in the heavenly realms *in Christ Jesus*, in order that in the coming ages he might show the incomparable riches of his grace, expressed *in his kindness* to us *in Christ Jesus*. For it is by grace you have been saved, through faith—and this not from yourselves, it is the gift of God—not by works, so that no one can boast. For we are God's handiwork, created *in Christ Jesus* to do good works, which God prepared in advance for us to do. (Emphasis added)

That's eight covenant phrases in just seven verses! Think he's trying to communicate something here? As if that's not enough, he tacks on six more covenant phrases in the next three verses.

> Therefore, remember that formerly you who are Gentiles by birth and called *"uncircumcised"* by those who call themselves *"the circumcision"* (which is done in the body by human hands)—remember that at that time you were *separate from Christ*, excluded from citizenship in Israel and *foreigners to the covenants of the promise*, without hope and without God in the world. But now *in Christ Jesus* you who once were far away have been brought near *by the blood of Christ*. (Vv. 11-13, emphasis added)

Circumcision under the Abrahamic covenant was the mark on the body that a male Israelite was in covenant with God. It was understood that his wife and daughters were included in the covenant under his covering.

Ceremonial Words

In terms of the formal requirements, we find covenant words like:

- Blessings
- Curses
- Oath
- Vows
- Swearing
- Treaty
- Testament

We see covenant language in Deuteronomy 28, which includes the pronouncement of blessings and curses we saw in the covenant ceremony. "Now it shall be, if you diligently obey the LORD your God, being careful to do all His commandments which I command you today, the LORD your God will set you high above all the nations of the earth. All these blessings will come upon you and overtake you if you obey the LORD your God" (vv. 1-2, NASB).

Verses 3-4 and 6-7 continue: "Blessed shall you be in the city, and blessed shall you be in the country. Blessed shall be the offspring of your body and the produce of your ground and the offspring of your beasts, the increase of your herd and the young of your flock. . . . Blessed shall you be when you come in, and blessed shall you be when you go out. The LORD shall cause your enemies who rise up against you to be defeated before you; they will come out against you one way and will flee before you seven ways" (NASB). When your enemies come to tamper with you, let them know who your covenant partner is. One of the blessings inherent in the covenant relationship is that we are partners with powerful and fearsome Almighty God.

The pronouncement of blessings is followed by the pronouncement of curses, a continuation of covenant language:

But it shall come about, if you do not obey the LORD your God, to observe to do all His commandments and His statutes with which I charge you today, that all these curses will come upon you and overtake you: Cursed shall you be in the city, and cursed shall you be in the country. Cursed shall be your basket and your kneading bowl. Cursed shall be the offspring of your body and the produce of your ground, the increase of your herd and the young of your flock. Cursed shall you be when you come in, and cursed shall you be when you go out. The LORD will send upon you curses, confusion, and rebuke, in all you undertake to do, until you are destroyed and until you perish quickly, on account of the evil of your deeds. . . . The LORD will smite you with consumption. (Vv. 15-20, 22, NASB)

The words "oath," "vows," and "swear" all essentially refer to the same covenantal context: the verbalization of the covenant promises and terms. These words are interchangeable in Scripture and should be taken very seriously when mentioned. In the book of Hebrews, which offers the most thorough commentary on the topic of covenant in the New Testament, God lays out the certainty of his promise concerning the Abrahamic covenant.

When God made his promise to Abraham, since there was no one greater for him to **swear by**, he **swore by himself**, saying, "I will surely **bless you** and give you many descendants." And so after waiting patiently, Abraham received what was **promised.** People **swear by** someone greater than themselves, and **the oath confirms** what is said and puts an end to all argument. Because God wanted to make the **unchanging nature** of his purpose very clear to **the heirs** of what was **promised,** he confirmed it with **an oath.** (Heb. 6:13-17, emphasis added)

The words "treaty" or "testament" are synonyms to the word "covenant" itself; hence, the Old and New Testaments that mark the two divisions of the Bible are also referred to as the old and new *covenants* in some versions.

Remember

The words "remember" and "remembrance" in the ancient Hebrew and Greek mind are completely different from today's Western thinking. "To remember" in the West describes the mental activity of not forgetting something that has once been placed in the mind, as if studying for an exam. It can also mean an attempt to recall something that happened in the long past as if it's a distant thought stuck deep in some cognitive fog inside our heads.

Neither of these definitions fully applies to the biblical and covenantal definition of the word "remember." If so, then the words of Jesus to his disciples on the night of the Last Supper were only meant specifically for those men around that table. We know this is not the case, so what does "remember" really mean?

In his book *The Lost Secret of the New Covenant*, Malcolm Smith notes that "remember" isn't just a mental activity but also "an activity of the whole person—spirit, mind, emotion, and body . . . it meant *to do* the past event, not merely *to think* about it. To remember meant to re-create the past event, bringing it into the present moment by reenacting it, employing rituals and symbols to do so."[1]

It is similar to when a husband and wife renew or "reenact" their wedding vows on their twenty-fifth anniversary. One Bible dictionary further states that to remember means that the persons remembering totally identified with and participated in all the powers and effects of the original event.[2] These accurate definitions of "remember" call on a person to actively look for ways to bless one's covenant partner. It means to take the initiative. Be proactive not reactive in honoring a covenant! This has immediate and practical application for all marriage covenants.

"Remember" also means Jesus was planting a double thought in his disciples' hearts that they would come to fully understand only after the resurrection. This instruction and subsequent revelation was profound: by taking Communion in order to remember him they would actually be able to both proclaim the Lord's death until he comes and also bring the power of the cross into their daily lives. It places tremendous value on the resurrection of Christ and blessed hope of our own bodily resurrection.

This has huge implications for the believer today. The Bible proclaims that by the stripes of Jesus inflicted on the cross our infirmities were taken up, our sorrows carried away, our peace was provided, and our wounds were healed (Isa. 53:4-5). Therefore, could it be there is a link between regular Communion participation and physical/emotional healing for the sick? Many believers have testified to this supernatural occurrence after specifically "remembering" the new covenant cut by Jesus Christ via the taking of the Communion elements.

When I (Rob) teach on covenant at my home church, I take one entire lesson on the covenant meal. After the teaching I pass out the elements to my students, but they are asked not to partake yet. I then announce I am about to play on a viewing screen several uninterrupted minutes of the climatic ending to the film *The Passion of the Christ*. They are instructed to take the Communion elements whenever they feel led by the Holy Spirit to do so as they watch the images of Jesus' death on the cross in the darkened room.

It is very common to notice people reduced to silent tears after reverently taking the Communion elements. The discussion afterward is usually loaded with emotional healing and revelation.

More on this word "remember" will be discussed in chapter 15 on the covenant meal.

SECTION II
OLD TESTAMENT COVENANTS

5

GOD'S FIRST COVENANTS WITH HUMANKIND

It doesn't seem fair or impartial. But it's the cold hard truth: the choice of disobedience from Adam and Eve created a mess for the rest of us.

And let's be even more honest: this wasn't a "fall" into a sin, which makes their decision sound like an accident where they somehow "slipped up." No, this was a leap into rebellion! Especially for Adam, who knew very well what he was doing when he ate of the tree. Eve may not have been quite as culpable, since the Scripture indicates she was deceived. But what was done had huge consequences.

Tragically, their choice at the tree of knowledge of good and evil plunged the entire human race into a natural separation from a perfect and sinless God, not just the two of them. A study of this familiar Sunday school story through the lens of covenant will help explain many of the words, actions, and descriptions of what happened in the garden of Eden. This is a story of a covenant established and then broken. It's painful to read because its aftermath still affects us to this day. Scholars and commentators call this first promise Adam's covenant, the Adamic covenant, the covenant of life, or the covenant of creation.

God created humanity to be his covenant partners. But why? The only answer to that is love. The undergirding meaning of creation is the love of God. I (Rob) was interviewing Malcolm Smith for a documentary on covenant, and during our conversation he raised a profound question, "What God is in his right mind would create another free will in the universe?" I sat silently and waited for him to answer his own question. He did. "Only love with the intent of having a reciprocal love. That would be the only reason to do it. But we're dealing with Creator-to-creature and also God knew it would be not only Creator-to-creature but Creator-to-rebel sinner! And therefore you have a covenant which is not only pure love, but also grace, mercy, longsuffering, forgiveness, reconciliation, many other expressions of love."[1]

And it all began to unfold in the garden.

Many of the covenant elements disclosed in chapter 3 actually made their first appearance in human history in the garden of Eden, not in the Hittite culture of Abraham's day. But because these steps of a covenant ceremony explained earlier in chapter 3 are so full and complete, they offer an easy yardstick by which to measure the presence of covenants made before and after the 2000 to 1500 BC time period. So what covenant elements do we find?

Adam's Covenant

The Representative: Adam is clearly defined in Romans 5:12 as a covenantal representative of the entire human race. We were "in" him as Adam walked in the garden. What happened to him and the decisions he made would set the tone for his descendants—just like how a covenant works. "Therefore, just as sin entered the world through one man, and death through sin, and in this way death came to all people, because all sinned." This is a distinctly covenantal concept that appears at the very dawn of human history.

Terms and Blessings/Curses: Four specific items can be identified.

- The first term of this covenant with Adam was to "Be fruitful, multiply, and fill the earth, and subdue it" (Gen. 1:28,

AMP). "Adam" means "humankind" in Hebrew and can be construed as God speaking to humankind in general, not just the first individual human being.

- God then instructs the first couple that they may eat whatever seed-bearing plant they desire. Adam was also informed that this covenant would require him to both tend (work) and also to guard (keep watch over) the garden of Eden. This covenant of life was not designed for humankind to enjoy some utopian vacation in the midst of breathtaking scenery. Production was required, not just consumption. Yet this work was designed to be extremely gratifying and pleasant to perform. The joy of the Lord would be their eternal strength. God was privileging this new creature made in his image to participate in the divine nature by engaging in the art of ecstatic creativity!

- The last term of this covenant God gave to Adam was that he was free to eat from any seed-bearing tree in the garden except for one: the Tree of the Knowledge of Good and Evil. If this term was violated, God said Adam would "die." The Hebrew word in Genesis 2:17 is *muwth*, which has several derivations of death, including "to die as a penalty." This aspect of the covenant term seems to indicate an amazing proposition had Adam done the opposite: if you don't eat this fruit, then you will live forever. What was God saying in this covenant offer? *Do you really trust that I am the Judge of what is good and what is evil, of what is right and what is wrong? Do you believe I am dispenser of true and faithful justice? Or do you think you should sit in this seat of judgment?*

These words were a warning from God. He was clearly communicating that he was the determiner of good and evil. It was never a burden that Adam was asked to bear. We see within these covenant terms a clear path to living under a blessing or under a curse. When our covenant representatives—Adam and Eve—failed to keep these terms, we were placed under the curse and consequence of sin, destined to die by being separated from the very source of Life.

Memorials: Two primary trees were planted by God (not by Adam) to be a reminder of this covenant. The **Tree of Life** was to serve as a visual reminder of the moment of initial conception when earth dust met the "breath of God" and humankind was given spirit-life. The inference from these early Genesis chapters points to the permission Adam and Eve had to eat from its fruit! Perhaps the continual eating of this tree's fruit gave them a kind of rechargeable energy that could have allowed their bodies to last forever. (That's a top-twenty question to ask God for sure when we arrive in his eternal presence!) There was no prohibition to eat this fruit until after sin entered the human race. After Genesis 3, the benefits of this Adamic covenant had been lost. Could humankind ever regain the status of being righteous in God's sight?

The **Tree of the Knowledge of Good and Evil** was to serve as a visual reminder that this covenant is actually conditional. In other words, humans have freedom of choice. Although, this is a second tree mentioned in Genesis 1, the important focus is not in the physical tree but what the tree represented. God could have selected something else to test humans. It could have been a restriction from some diving into a nearby pond or climbing a mountain. But God chose a tree. Imagine if our Bible had read "the mountain of the knowledge of good and evil"! Regardless of the method that presented the choice, humans must decide continually to remain in the covenant relationship or cast it off. As explained earlier, this tree was tied into one of the terms of the Adamic covenant.

Blood Sacrifice: This element actually appears in Scripture immediately after Adam and Eve broke the covenant! Sort of. It can be argued that God already had this element tucked away in "the Lamb who was slain from the creation of the world" (Rev. 13:8). Either way, God took the initiative! He, not Adam, killed an animal (or animals) and made garments of skin for the world's only two inhabitants. Two covenant breakers. Two people desperately loved by God. A compassionate "greater LORD" who had to find a way to symbolically "cover the sin" as a spiritual "IOU" for the "lesser lord" (Adam) until the Lamb of God would come to "take away sin" forever from the heart of humans.

It's quite an amazing thought, really. The first blood that was shed on the planet after Adam and Eve were created was at the hand of God, and it was covenant blood! Their nakedness indicated innocence and purity before the fall. Now dominated by sin, their physical bodies needed to be covered by something that had died. This was a way of symbolically covering their sin until the true and final Lamb would come that would take away their sin.

It's unlikely that they fully understood covenant at that moment, but it's where a blood covenant was first seen with the human eye. Since Adam lived 930 years, he told the story to his children, grandchildren, great-grandchildren, and so on.[2]

Although it cannot be proven, it is very likely that this animal was actually a lamb. These animals willingly go to slaughter. They don't fight or resist when captured. They are gentle and meek. They would be the primary animal used for sacrifices later under the Sinaitic covenant in Israel. And one of Jesus' titles incorporates this animal: the Lamb of God.

A Serpent's Smooth-Forked Tongue

God has many names by which he reveals himself to humankind. But several are used more than others. The typical name to describe God's title of deity is the Hebrew word Elohim. This is the word used for God during the creation account in Genesis. It speaks about him as Ruler, Sovereign, Judge, and Creator. But beginning in Genesis 2 another name is added. He is called the "LORD God." What does this word mean and why was it added? Surely not just to break up the monotony of using one word. It was a very intentional addition. The word "LORD" in Hebrew in these early chapters is "Yahweh" (from the infinitive "to be") and is generally confirmed later in Scripture as the personal covenant name of God. It speaks about him as Friend, Lover, Comforter, and even Father.

With this covenantal backdrop, it is actually mystifying to think about humankind's choice to sin. It was spiritual suicide, and they knew it. They knew what God had said and still they did it. They had everything! They had absolute authority. Absolute provision. They had no concept of a need! The only possible temptation was to arouse envy toward the one Person who is greater than himself. The only thing humans don't have is the ability to become as God himself.

Eve was deceived by a small creature that she had been given full authority over. A speaking snake! That should have aroused suspicion. An animal on the ground suddenly speaking in a vocal language they understood? Weird, huh? There is no evidence to believe otherwise, that the serpent just somehow put thoughts into Eve's mind. There was an actual conversation happening.

Have we ever thought of how the tone of the conversation played out? If you were Satan, how would you have tempted Eve? Where would you have done it? How would you have presented the fruit for eating? How would he have referred to God? By asking these questions, we discover an amazing truth of how Satan attempted to mask the *covenant nature* of God. He passionately intends—then and now—to distort and misrepresent the covenant.

In Genesis 3, the third person narrator of the account uses the words "LORD God," which translates as Yahweh Elohim. Let's break those two words down. Yahweh is the personal covenant name of God. Elohim speaks more to God as Creator, Sovereign, Ruler, and Judge. It is in Satan's first recorded words that we discover he has hatched a devious plan. *If I can just get this woman to temporarily omit her awareness of God as a covenant partner and focus only on him as an overseer, then I may have a chance to plunge her and her husband into the curse. Just maybe I can raise enough suspicion and envy to persuade them to eat the forbidden fruit.*

Note carefully what happens in Genesis 3:1-3: "Now the serpent was more crafty than any of the wild animals the LORD God had made. He said to the woman, 'Did God really say, "You must not eat from any tree in the garden"?' The woman said to the serpent, 'We may eat from the trees in the garden, but God did say, "You must not eat fruit from the tree that is in the middle of the garden."'"

Satan omits the covenant name of God, calling him just Elohim! His plan gets off to a good start. Eve answered this slithering creature with the same name of Elohim, not Yahweh Elohim in her response! He convinced her to ignore the covenant nature of a loving God at the beginning of the conversation, appealing to just his rulership and sovereignty.

Satan knew the power of covenant and desired to mask it, avoid it, and even disregard it. Tragically, Eve fell for his ruse. Look again at the passage above. She omits the covenant name of Yahweh in her answer! She refers to deity as just God instead of LORD God. Satan now had Eve on unstable ground, and she didn't even realize it. Without her covenant "filter" on, Eve was vulnerable and ripe for deception, even if just for moment. And a moment would be all that the serpent needed.

This exchange is similar to the conversation in the film *Star Wars* when Obi Wan Kenobi uses the Force to plant a thought in the mind of an unsuspecting storm trooper. "These aren't the droids you're looking for," Kenobi suggests when his party is stopped by the Republic's army. The storm trooper pauses a moment before saying, "These aren't the droids we're looking for." A funny moment in the fictional movie, but not so humorous in the garden of Eden.

Satan continues to omit the covenant name of Yahweh twice in his response: "'You will not certainly die,' the serpent said to the woman. 'For God knows that when you eat from it your eyes will be opened, and you will be like God, knowing good and evil'" (Gen. 3:4-5). The rest of the story ends in Eve's deception into sin and Adam's disobedience into sin.

יהוה
YHWH

As a prophetic sidebar to the story, the Hebrew letters for Yahweh are YHWH (Yod-Hey-Vav-Hey). Scholars call this the Tetragrammaton name of God. These are the four letters that symbolize God (tetra = four, grammaton = written). In a later chapter you will see something amazing tucked inside the definition of each of these Hebrew letters when put together—an encrypted message that points directly to the new covenant in Jesus Christ.

Noah's Covenant

Noah's name in Hebrew means "This one shall give us rest." His father, Lamech, thought Noah might be the promised one to deliver them from the curse of sin's weariness and toil.

The covenant with Noah, documented primarily in Genesis 6 and 9, is also called the covenant of preservation because its divine promises prevented a second aquatic destruction of the earth and its inhabitants. This cataclysmic event demands investigation. Was it an approaching and unstoppable act of nature? Was it a necessary global bath the world needed to reestablish its ecological imbalance? Was God just throwing a holy temper tantrum? None of these notions offer a salient answer. The key is found in a prophecy in Genesis 3:15 shortly after the rebellion into sin. God foretold that Eve's seed would one day crush the head of the serpent. The term "head" symbolizes the serpent's newfound "authority" over the human race since humankind had just relinquished it through disobedience.

As time passed, humanity slid deeper into sin. Eve's "seed" or offspring became so utterly polluted that the fulfillment of this prophecy seemed impossible; the serpent appeared to have an unshakable grip on humankind. The Scripture says that

the Lord saw how great the wickedness of the human race had become on the earth, and that every inclination of the thoughts of the human heart was only evil all the time. The LORD regretted that he had made human beings on the earth, and his heart was deeply troubled. So the LORD said, "I will wipe from the face of the earth the human race I have created—and with them the animals, the birds and the creatures that move along the ground—for I regret that I have made them." But Noah found favor in the eyes of the LORD. (Gen. 6:5-8)

Will God's prophecy die on the vine? He must still have access into a purely human race to redeem a purely human race. Enter the flood. Enter the Noahic covenant.

The Representative: Noah is clearly defined in Genesis 6:18 as a covenantal representative of the entire human race before the flood began. We were "in him" as he entered the ark. God reiterates this point after the waters subsided in Genesis 9:9-10: "I now establish my covenant with you and with your descendants after you and with every living creature that was with you." It is interesting to note that even those specific animals in the ark were defined as covenant representatives of their species.

Terms and Blessings/Curses: Four specific items can be identified.

- Noah and his family, and two of every kind of animal shall enter the ark for preservation.
- Noah and his family are instructed to be fruitful and multiply (a repeat of the Adamic covenant).
- In addition to eating seed-bearing plants, these humans and their descendants may now eat meat.
- Capital punishment is permitted if a person's lifeblood is taken.

Blood Sacrifice: Noah was instructed to take seven "clean" animals instead of just two of each kind. He ordered the same for all birds. Noah knew exactly why, and he performed his appropriate response in Genesis 8:20 after the flood was over. "Then Noah built an altar to the LORD and, taking some of all the clean animals and clean birds, he sacrificed burnt offerings on it."

Noah was offering a blood sacrifice as part of this covenant! In every covenant-making ceremony the shedding of blood occurs. Notice it wasn't until after he performed this ritual that God announced the oaths of his covenant promise of preservation.

Oaths/Vows: "The LORD smelled the pleasing aroma and said in his heart: 'Never again will I curse the ground because of humans, even though every inclination of the human heart is evil from childhood. And never again will I destroy all living creatures as I have done" (Gen. 8:21-22). He further went on to describe a new type of weather cycle and harvesting season for the earth. This is likely because of the relationship of the earth to the sun. No more firmament, or vaporous protection like a greenhouse, was positioned between the sun and the earth. Perhaps even the earth's tilt axis angle had changed as a result of this catastrophic event.

Memorial: We still enjoy the memorial of God's covenant with Noah to this day. It is the rainbow in the sky during or after a rain shower.

And God said, "This is the sign of the covenant I am making between me and you and every living creature with you, a covenant for all generations to come: I have set my rainbow in the clouds, and it will be the sign of the covenant between me and the earth. Whenever I bring clouds over the earth and the rainbow appears in the clouds, I will remember my covenant between me and you and all living creatures of every kind. Never again will the waters become a flood to destroy all life. Whenever the rainbow appears in the clouds, I will see it and remember the everlasting covenant between God and all living creatures of every kind on the earth." (Gen. 9:12-16)

The Hebrew word that is translated in Genesis 9 as "rainbow" is literally the word for a warrior's bow. God often appears in Scripture as a warrior with his bow poised to render judgment. But now consider the rainbow set in the clouds: the warrior's bow is not held up in the position of warfare and judgment with arrows ready to fly, but at the side in the position of peace. The rainbow, set in the clouds, in the position of peace, reminds us of God's covenant with creation—a covenant in which God promises to maintain the created order.[3]

The colors arching in a half circle upward also remind us of his faithfulness to humankind and his ultimate intention to establish his kingdom of peace on the earth. We know this to be true because of the evidence of a similar rainbow of colors near the throne of God in Revelation 4.

A Repeating Pattern

Imagine that instead of books, chapters, and verses, you simply had one big, long, continuous document. Picture it: no verse numberings, no chapter numberings, and no books, such as Genesis, Exodus, and so forth. If that were the case, how would you understand the Bible? How would you make any sense out of it? How would you be able to find anything?

It would be difficult. However, there would be a pattern that would emerge as you began to process the document. As you began reading the Bible, you would suddenly notice something. You would discover that the Bible is comprised of several contracts or agreements or covenants. You would first observe that God made a contract or covenant with Adam. But as you read further, you would discover that God made another contract with Noah. As you continued reading, you would discover another contract or covenant; this time it was with Abraham. And as you kept reading you would find another one with Moses. And then one with David. And then you would discover a "new" covenant. Suddenly it would dawn on you. The Bible is comprised of six covenants. But as you studied them more, you would discover that three of them all fit together as one covenant (Abraham, David, and the "new"). Thus you would discover there were not six covenants as you originally thought but only four:

- Adam's covenant
- Noah's covenant

- Moses' covenant
- and the Abraham-David-new ("new" referring to Jesus) covenant

The Bible cannot be understood unless one grasps the covenants and the covenant-making ceremony. It is only then that the intentionality of the writers makes sense. We know this is strong language, but allow us to repeat it: One cannot understand the message of the Scriptures unless one grasps the four covenants that form the foundation of the biblical account.

Before exploring in detail the remainder of God's covenants with humankind, notice how all the covenants are positioned across history . . . and eternity.

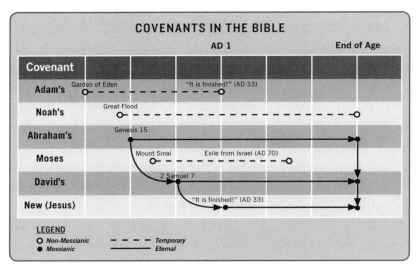

Fig. 5.1. Major Covenants in the Bible

The chart in figure 5.1 offers a unique perspective of God's covenants with humankind. Three covenants do not offer salvation in its terms/stipulations (Adam's, Noah's, and Moses'). The other three covenants do have humanity's spiritual salvation embedded in some fashion within its promises (Abraham's, David's, and new). The covenant panorama depicted is testimony to an expanding inclusion of humanity beyond the boundaries of people groups (Jew and Gentile), gender differences, and other human categories.

The lines in Figure 1 connect the Abrahamic covenant to the Davidic covenant to the new covenant because they are all essentially the unfolding extension of the same covenant birthed in the everlasting covenant (see chapter 12). This can also be understood as a "renewing" of a covenant, a common possibility in other human-to-human covenants throughout world history and in the Bible.

The Abrahamic covenant promised that there would be a Seed through Abraham's descendants that would bless the entire earth. This word "Seed" is capitalized in Scripture to indicate the singular, definitive, and final person who would redeem humanity through a later covenant. But who would it be and how would he be revealed? Fourteen generations later (in David's time), Abraham's descendants likely numbered in the tens of thousands. No further revelation from God had been unveiled until he prophesied that this Seed would come through David's family lineage. The Seed line had been further identified! And in the process God had eliminated thousands of other potential candidates living in the lands of Israel.

Furthermore, David was informed that the Seed would never fail to rule as King over the house of Israel. After fourteen more generations, David's physical descendants also likely numbered in the tens of thousands. And as before, no further revelation from God had been sent until the day he sent an angel to speak to a young peasant girl from Nazareth.

He then sent the actual Seed, Jesus the Son of God himself. His parents, Joseph and Mary, were both physical descendants of David, although through different sons of David. Joseph came through the line of Solomon and Mary came through the line of Nathan. More will be said about this in chapter 9 when we dissect David's covenant.

The result is what Jesus would call the new covenant. The word "new" in Greek is *kainos*, which means "of a new kind, unprecedented, novel, uncommon, unheard of." Why did Jesus use this word? *Because for the first time in the history of covenant-cutting, a single person would be both the covenant representative and the covenant sacrifice at the same time.*

This is unquestionably an "unprecedented and unheard of" type of covenant. It's as if God was saying, "I'm going to blow your mind with what I have planned for you!"

Jeremiah prophesied there would be a "new" covenant one day (Jer. 31:31). The Hebrew word he used for new is *chadash*, which also means "fresh." But he could never have imagined the unique way this would be fulfilled many centuries later.

So, the Abrahamic covenant extends into the Davidic covenant, which extends into the new covenant of Jesus Christ. And all three are unique expressions of the everlasting covenant! But how did Abram (later changed to Abraham) first encounter the offer of this amazing, covenant-making God? What kind of mistakes did Abram make along the way? And what did Abram do that ultimately labeled him the "friend of God" in the book of James and several other places in Scripture?

It's an incredible story filled with many twists and turns, including the possibility that Abram's father Terah was first given the covenant offer but failed to overcome a crippling addiction to a pagan deity. The next chapter is a tell-all exposé on the life and times of the man many refer to as "the father of our faith."

6

ABRAHAM'S COVENANT

Imagine if American music had a radio station based in Ur of the Chaldees circa 2000 BC. It would be pretty easy to predict the local DJ's song list. Tunes like "Blue Moon" by the Marcels, "Moon River" by Louis Armstrong, and "Man on the Moon" by R.E.M. would enjoy many frequent plays. They were infatuated with the moon.

In fact, they worshipped it.

Archaeological digs reveal Ur was undoubtedly a regional center of moon worship in the Middle East during Abram's day. Crescent moon symbols littered the streets. On statues, temples, seal impressions, pottery, clay tablets, weights, stone murals, jewelry, coins. Many of these discoveries were made by noted archaeologists G. Caton Thompson, Carleton S. Coon, Wendell Phillips, W. F. Albright, Richard Bower, and many others.[1]

Canaan or Bust

Raised by his father, Terah, Abram grew up in this culture. So let's just come out and say it: Abraham, the father of our Christian faith, was once a bona fide moon worshipper. How did he escape such idolatry to become the key figure in the entire Old Testament?

Genesis 11:31 through 12:5 suggests that Terah first heard the call of God to go to the land of Canaan, not Abram. In that culture, it was not generally accepted that a son could have received a greater revelation of God than his father.[2] But when the family reaches the upper city of Haran, they stop and settle there until Terah dies. This can be a very puzzling verse, unless we understand what lies inside Haran and what likely remains inside Terah's heart.

Both Haran and Terah had an unquenchable love to worship the moon. Perhaps Terah had visited Haran in earlier years. Perhaps he was very fond of this city and its moon worshipping fervor. We do know that Terah named one of his sons Haran. Was it in tribute to this city? Whatever the case, Abram's journey to Canaan was aborted by his father. After Terah's death, the mantle of the Canaan quest was passed down to Abram in Genesis 12:1: "Go from your country, your people and your father's household to the land I will show you." He continued down southward toward Canaan, picking up a servant named Eliezer in the city of Damascus.

Abram got tangled in several adventures before God directly spoke to him again. These included a trip out of Canaan to Egypt during a famine and dumping his wife, Sarai, to an Egyptian lord to save his own skin. Abram is definitely not the picture of God's man of faith and power when we first meet him! But he also had some bright moments.

He initiated a dramatic rescue mission to save his nephew Lot, built two altars to the Lord (not the moon god), and he took an oath (a covenant-type word) to a deity he called "the LORD, God Most High, Creator of heaven and earth" (Gen. 14:22).

It was Abraham's specific act of taking an oath out of fear and reverence to God that triggered the Lord to initiate the covenant. We, like Abram, must first embrace a holy reverence for God before he will tell us anything about covenant. The psalmist David saw this truth a thousand years later. "The friendship of the LORD is for those who fear him, and he makes his covenant known to them" (Ps. 25:14, NRSV).

The Smell of Blood in the Air

In Genesis 15, the Abrahamic covenant kicks into gear. God announces himself as Abram's shield and great reward. The Hebrew word for shield is "El Shaddai," which means "mighty mountain." But it also means "the breasted one." God was speaking Abram's visual language as a goat herder who for years had watched young goats suck at their mothers' breasts for nourishment and sustenance. Abram is thrilled at this new revelation but still has no idea how God will make him into a great nation since he has no children. So Abram decides to try and help God out.

How many times do we do the same?

Abram mentions that he has made Eliezer of Damascus his heir. A servant as an heir? God shakes his head and tells him he will have a son from his own body one day. Abram learns his own seed will be the heir! This is going to require a major step of faith since Abram is already about seventy-six years old, but this time he is ready to believe God's word.

In Genesis 15:6 we encounter one of the most important verses in the entire Bible. "Abram believed the Lord, and he credited it to him as righteousness." Let's break down what happened here.

The word "believe" means to "trust in, cling to, adhere to, rely upon." That's superglue type faith. That's "I ain't lettin' go" bulldog-tenacity faith.

The word "credited" can also be translated "reckoned," both of which mean "to pay into one's account wages that have not been earned."

The word "righteousness" means "to be in right standing with." It's like the currency required to be square with God.

So let's reconstruct this amazing sentence: Abram clung to God's covenant word, and the result was that a safe friendship with him was deposited as good currency into Abram's spiritual account. Abram now has a right standing with God not based on performance but based on his having surrendered completely to God.

That now established, one would think Abram would settle firmly into this relationship with God. He didn't. Abram reveals he now has more trouble believing in the promise of land than believing for a biological son! He asks God how can he be sure that he will inherit the land? Remember, at this point God has never specifically mentioned a covenant. He has only opened his mouth and said words to Abram.

God speaks again. He tells Abram to go fetch some animals and birds. A heifer, a goat, a ram, a dove, and a pigeon to be exact. A spark goes off in Abram's heart. He immediately knows what is about to happen!

A blood covenant!

No instructions are needed. Abram knows instantly what to do with them. He kills them, splits them in half, and spreads them across the desert floor. "This 'LORD, God Most High, Creator of heaven and earth' is going to cut a blood covenant with me!" Abram is energized and focused, driving away the inevitable vultures that arrive shortly after the smell of blood fills the air. They circle around the animal corpses, then nose-dive. Abram swats away every attack. Nothing is going to steal this covenant away from him.

God then puts him to sleep, and his eyes are opened to see a very strange vision that seems to mix both spiritual and physical worlds. The Scriptures seem to indicate that Abram, while in a deep sleep, is given eyes to see what looks like a blazing torch and a smoking pot pass back and forth between the animals split in half. What is happening here? God is engaging in one of the covenant steps: the walk of death as he passes between the two pieces of open flesh!

God is serving as the covenant representative both on his own behalf and on behalf of Abram. God is essentially making covenant with himself and including Abram and his descendants in the terms/blessings of the covenant.

Abram will never have to say "this covenant is depending on me to keep it." Again, it must be stressed: Abram makes no covenant promises or oaths! God does it all. Abram's only response is the "yes" of faith, and he just did that earlier that day because he "believed the LORD" and it was "credited . . . to him as righteousness." This is the heart of the Abrahamic covenant. It is locked into God's initiative, not humanity's.

An amazing truth begins to dawn on Abram: faith in this Abrahamic covenant means God is saying, "You, Abram, get out of the way; I will do it for you and as you. It's in my name. I'm walking through those pieces making vows, not you. All you need to do is make your response of belief!"

Sarah Submits to Covenant Faith

But after the euphoria of the presence of the blood covenant ceremony, Abram slips back into trusting himself. Sarai still can't get pregnant. Abram can't figure out what's going on. Maybe it's Sarai's barren womb. After all, God said a child would come from Abram's seed. Sarai feels Abram's pain and offers a plan. The problem is that it was a custom of the contemporary culture, not a God-idea. She offers Abram the services of her maidservant Hagar.

Hagar gets pregnant. Abram is elated. Ishmael is born. It appears the covenant is now on its way to the next generation!

God says nothing.

For thirteen years.

In Genesis 17, God finally opens his mouth again. Abram is now ninety-nine years old. God announces a name change for Abram to Abraham and also that he must undergo circumcision. Circumcision is to be the physical sign (or mark on the body) of the covenant partnership between God and Abraham and all those who will follow under Abraham. Quite a shock on both accounts for a man almost a century old! Sarai's name will change too. It will become Sarah. But then the real zinger in verse 16: God announces that she will have a son.

Are you kidding me? Abraham's faith has reached its limit. *Uh, God . . . she's ninety!* He tries to reason. "If only Ishmael might live under your blessing!" (Gen. 17:18). But God is not interested in Abraham's ideas. *No Eliezers or Ishmaels needed, my covenant friend Abraham!*

When three strange visitors meet Abraham later in Genesis 18, they sit down and share a meal. The number three in Scripture naturally tends to indicate the presence of the Lord as the Trinity Godhead (Father, Son, and Holy Spirit). Regardless of whether Abraham knows about the Trinity, he senses they are representing the Lord God himself. *Perhaps these three beings are angels? I must treat them with utmost respect!* They give a message over the meal. Sarah will give birth in a year. Sarah laughs. The men, now just called "The Lord" till the end of the story (Abraham was right), catch her chuckling behind the tent. "Is anything too hard for the Lord?" they ask her (v. 14). It is her moment. She, too, must enter into the hilarious dance of covenant faith in the impossible.

Sarah must have believed after the Lord's presence left. She and Abraham "tried again." It worked this time. She conceived.

Sarah probably chuckled again when she knew she was pregnant. Perhaps several tears of joy were mixed in with her laughter. God's choice for her son's name was perfect. Isaac in Hebrew means "laughter."

The Breath of God

Before moving on to the rest of the details of the Abrahamic covenant, we need to go back and carefully examine this name change. Remember, name changes were common in covenant making. But why the change from Abram to Abraham? Doesn't seem like much of an alteration, really. If you're going to change someone's name, why not make wholesale changes? Why just the addition of essentially one brief syllable in the middle of the original name? Our first clue should be to understand the Hebrew definitions of both the old and new name. Abram means "exalted father" while Abraham means "father of many." This is a start but doesn't really tell the whole story. After all, the word "father" still appears in both names. The term "Abraham" seems to be just a type of multiplication of the name "Abram."

God includes the covenantal rite of a name exchange in his covenant with Abram. He is putting the central sound of his name, Yahweh, inside the new name of his covenant partner. No longer shall he be called Abram. He shall be called AbrAHam! But God doesn't stop there. He gives himself another name too. From as early as Genesis 26, Yahweh begins referring to himself as the "God of Abraham." A complete name blending has taken place in the Abrahamic covenant!

At this point putting on our covenant filter will be helpful. In the Old Testament no one word adequately describes God. There are multiple names for him, each of which depicts a feature or an aspect of his character. The one used in Genesis 15 is "Yahweh," which we commonly read as "Jehovah." "Yahweh" means "the oath-making God" or "the oath-keeping God." God is the original promise keeper. He is the covenant maker and the covenant keeper.

In ancient Hebrew there were no vowels—only consonants. The letter "a" in "Yahweh" is a pronunciation aid that was added later. God's name is spelled YHWH in the Hebrew Tetragrammaton. The central sound in this name Yahweh sounds like an "H" in the English lexicon. This is similar to a deep breath being expelled from the body's diaphragm. When God made covenant with Abram, he put the "H" from his name into Abraham's name and changed Sarai's name to "Sarah." The Hebrew letter "H" is the sound of breath, generally signifying the breath or presence of God.[3]

In Genesis 1 we read about the creation of man and woman. When God made Adam from the dust, the first man was merely a body. What made Adam live? The breath of God. We see the same concept in the New Testament. The Holy Spirit is called the

"Holy *Pneuma*" in Greek. *Pneuma* means wind; literally it means *the holy puff of breath of God.*

Could it be that when God hovered over the still lifeless molecules of a man's body in the garden of Eden that he breathed his own name, "Yahweh," into the nostrils of Adam in order to impart life? Imagine that. God expelling the sound of the covenantal name of "YaHHHHHweh" over man and the result being life into that pile of "red dirt." That's a question to ask God in heaven one day, right?

So we can see the significance of the letter that symbolizes breath being put in the middle of Abram's name as a symbol that God is his covenant partner. Abram becomes Abr*AH*am. In fact, the relationship is so meaningful that the author of 2 Chronicles, when talking to God, calls Abraham "Your friend" (2 Chron. 20:7). God refers to him as "My friend" in Isaiah 41:8, and James calls him "the friend of God" (James 2:23, NASB).

As we have seen, God also took Abraham's name. Throughout Scripture, time after time, God calls himself "the God of Abraham." Attached to God's title is the name of this man, his covenant partner. The covenantal step of the name exchange has now been completed.

"Now I Know"—God

Scripture is silent on exactly how many years later it was, but the time came when Isaac was now a young man. Some suggest that he was around thirty-three years of age,[4] though that is impossible to verify. It was time for the ultimate test of Abraham's faith. It would also be an equal test for Isaac himself.

In Genesis 22, God told Abraham to sacrifice his covenant son on an altar as a burnt offering: "Some time later God tested Abraham. He said to him, 'Abraham!' 'Here I am,' he replied" (v. 1). He was then instructed to kill Isaac and then burn the body. It made absolutely no sense. This was the child of covenant promise! What is God thinking? But this time Abraham was silent. He didn't say, "If only Isaac might live under your blessing!" as he had said about Ishmael many years earlier. This was a different Abraham—a man whose faith had now completely abandoned itself to God's plan and purposes. He now understood the requirement to exchange firstborn sons to "prove" the covenant.

He begins the journey as instructed. Mount Moriah. Three days' journey. Wood. Offering. Sacrifice. Blood. Death . . . Trust.

What Abraham didn't fully understand at the time was how God was engaging in the final and ultimate step in covenant making: the exchange of the oldest child. Tradition stated that in order to "seal" the agreement, to prove the covenant was for real, the partners would exchange oldest sons. The sons would actually move into the home of the partner to be raised. It was a painful event, but one that would prove the covenant was for real. *Where was God's Son? Was there even such a thing?* Abraham had no clue. It didn't matter at the moment.

Eventually Isaac asked his father where they would get the animal they were to sacrifice. "Yahweh Jireh," Abraham answered. "God will provide." Abraham bound his son and placed him on the wood. Isaac didn't fight it. No conversation between father and son are recorded in Scripture at this pivotal moment. It was too painful to talk. Their joint faith filled the atmosphere. No words were needed.

The moment of truth arrived; Abraham raised the knife. That's when God arrested him and told him to stop. "Now I know that you fear God, because you have not withheld from me your son, your only son" (Gen. 22:12).

Hebrews 11:17 tells us that in his heart Abraham had already figuratively sacrificed Isaac. Genesis 22:4 notes that "on the third day Abraham looked up and saw the place in the distance." In other words, in Abraham's heart Isaac had, figuratively speaking, already been dead for three days since that was the length of the journey. God "resurrected him," again *figuratively*, on the third day. "By faith Abraham, when he was tested, offered up Isaac, and he who had received the promises was offering up his only begotten son" (Heb. 11:17, NASB). How could Abraham do this?

Scripture gives us a glimpse into Abraham's thinking. Isaac was his only son. Yet Abraham knew that God had promised him that his descendants would come through the line of Isaac and outnumber the stars in heaven. Hebrews 11:19 states: "He considered that God is able to raise people even from the dead" (NASB).

Abraham's confidence in the covenant-keeping God was so great that he believed God would give Isaac back to him through resurrection. In effect God, when he stopped Abraham from sacrificing Isaac, was saying, "Abraham, I've seen your heart. It's as if you've already sacrificed him. You know that I would have to resurrect him since he's the 'promised child.' And your confidence in me is so great, you really believe I'll do exactly that, so let's save both of us some time. You don't need to go any further in this ceremony. Stop now. Lay down the knife. You've already passed the test."

Genesis 22:16-17a says, "By Myself I have sworn, declares the LORD, *because you have done this thing* [What thing? Sacrificed Isaac] *and have not withheld your son*, your only son, indeed I will greatly bless you" (NASB, emphasis added). God goes on to promise Abraham many offspring: "Your seed shall possess the gate of their enemies. In your seed all the nations of the earth shall be blessed" (vv. 17c-18, NASB).

God was in effect saying, "Abraham, since you have sacrificed your son, I am now required by covenant commitment to do the same for you. You have tested and proven yourself to be faithful to our covenant. It will stand!"

Ultimately this exchange of the oldest male child would be paralleled in the sacrifice of Jesus. This is the powerful, revolutionary truth of the new covenant.

More than a Coincidence

This moment in history cannot be overstated. Do we realize what happened here? *For the first time in human history, a man's action has put God himself under covenant obligation!* God was now compelled (by covenant) to send Jesus his one and only Son to the earth for Abraham and his descendants. This is a staggering truth and stands as the reason for the importance of the Abrahamic covenant as a direct link to the new covenant in Christ.

The parallels between their two sons are striking.

- Isaac and Jesus both rode to the place of their sacrifice on donkeys.
- Isaac and Jesus both carried wood to the sacrifice (the Hebrew word for tree means wood).
- Isaac was a "dead man" in the heart of Abraham for three days. Jesus was a "dead man" in the plan of God for three days.
- Isaac traveled to Mount Moriah. That place today is called Mount Calvary, a rocky hill just outside Jerusalem where Jesus traveled to his sacrifice.
- Isaac is tested and must now embrace his father's faith. He allows himself to be bound on wood. "Abraham answered, 'God himself will provide the lamb for the burnt offering, my son.' And the two of them went on together" (Gen. 22:8). Jesus is tested and must embrace his Father's faith. He allows himself to be bound on wood. "Nevertheless, not my will, but yours, be done" (Luke 22:42, ESV). And later: "Father, into your hands I commit my spirit" (23:46).

Summary of the Steps

To review, we can identify the following covenant steps in the Abrahamic covenant:

Representative: God represented both himself and Abram through the blazing torch and smoking pot.

Terms and Blessings/Curses: Two passages in particular stand out. The first is Genesis 12:2-3: "I will make you into a great nation. I will bless you and make you famous, and you will be a blessing to others. I will bless those who bless you and curse those who treat you with contempt. All the families on earth will be blessed through you" (NLT).

The second is Genesis 15:18-21: "So the LORD made a covenant with Abram that day and said, 'I have given this land to your descendants, all the way from the border of Egypt to the great Euphrates River—the land now occupied by the Kenites, Kenizzites, Kadmonites, Hittites, Perizzites, Rephaites, Amorites, Canaanites, Girgashites, and Jebusites'" (NLT).

Note that there are no curses in this covenant!

Blood Sacrifice: The animals from Genesis 15 can be viewed as the initial blood sacrifice that established the covenant. But it's also fair to say that in order to keep the Abrahamic covenant, the blood of Jesus Christ as God's only Son had to be shed as well.

Mark on the Body: The rite of circumcision of Abraham and his descendants. This was later abolished when the Abrahamic covenant was fulfilled in the new covenant. The apostle Paul says that the important mark or seal now is not physical circumcision but rather a spiritual circumcision on the heart (Col. 2:11).

Oaths/Vows: "This is what the LORD says: Because you have obeyed me and have not withheld even your son, your only son, I swear by my own name that I will certainly bless you. I will multiply your descendants beyond number, like the stars in the sky and the sand on the seashore. Your descendants will conquer the cities of their enemies. And through your descendants all the nations of the earth will be blessed—all because you have obeyed me" (Gen. 22:16-18, NLT).

Exchange of Names: Abram's name was changed to Abraham, and the Lord added a new name to himself—the God of Abraham.

Exchange of Oldest Male Child: They exchanged sons in Isaac and Jesus.

Meal: This meal is found in Genesis 18 with the three visitors who were symbolic of the Lord's presence.

Memorials: While there was no official memorial established, it is notable that Mount Moriah and Mount Calvary share the same physical location just outside the city walls of Jerusalem. Many scholars also believe this may be the Place of the Skull or Golgotha: a site still honored today by Christians visiting the Holy Land.

So we see that the Abrahamic covenant flows into the new covenant. Or put it another way: the new covenant is an extension of the Abrahamic covenant. One day Jesus was talking with Jewish religious leaders about the validity of his ministry in relation their validity as children of Abraham. They attempted to trap Jesus when they asked him, "Are you greater than our father Abraham? He died, and so did the prophets. Who do you think you are?" (John 8:53).

One of Jesus' responses often gets overlooked in Scripture. "Abraham rejoiced at the thought of seeing my day; he saw it and was glad" (v. 56). This is a stunning verse! Abraham knew one day that a man from his family would be the Messiah. He may not have known that the Messiah's name would be Jesus or that he would be born to a peasant family in Bethlehem, but he saw the Savior through covenant faith in God. And he rejoiced.

"You are not yet fifty years old . . . and you have seen Abraham!" the Jewish leaders answered in their spiritual blindness. "'Very truly I tell you,' Jesus answered, 'before Abraham was born, I am!'" (vv. 57-58). It was a very intentional and controversial comment Jesus knew he had to declare. Those words planted the seed that led to his eventual crucifixion.

7

MOSES' COVENANT

Ever wonder what Bible characters looked like in real life? Take Moses, for example. Does your mental picture of him somehow always end up looking like . . . Charlton Heston? You're not alone. It's a safe bet to say that most American Christians connect Moses and the Ten Commandments to Heston and Cecile B. DeMille's famous 1956 film. *The Ten Commandments* unpacks a fairly accurate detail of the account of Israel's exodus from Egypt and early history in the wilderness. But the film does not instruct audiences on the details of God's covenant heart for the sons and daughters of Abraham.

It's also probably a good bet Moses didn't look much like an American movie star.

A Covenant Unlike Any Other in the Bible

The covenant with Moses, also called the Mosaic or Sinaitic covenant, is the most detailed covenant we have in the Bible. More than the Abrahamic covenant and even more than the new covenant. It is this covenant (not the Abrahamic covenant) that is referred to as the old covenant or Old Testament, which makes up nearly two-thirds of the entire Bible after the early church fathers divided the Scriptures into two parts.

Out of the 286 references to the word "covenant" in the Old Testament, 150 of them concern this Sinaitic covenant. It is often called Sinaitic only because it was founded on Mount Sinai when Moses represented the entire family of Israel. The first five books of the Bible (Genesis, Exodus, Leviticus, Numbers, and Deuteronomy), called the Torah and traditionally attributed primarily to Moses, deal very specifically with the Sinaitic covenant and the history surrounding it.

These writings were held in such high regard that young Jewish boys training for a spot as a future rabbi had to memorize the entire Torah to even be considered. Torah in Hebrew means "teaching, instruction, or law," and it is full of stories, rules, and rituals Israel had to follow in order to maintain covenant fidelity with God.

That's right. People had to labor at keeping it. This covenant was not just Abraham sitting in the corner watching God walk through the bloody bodies of split-open animals promising to keep the covenant on behalf of both parties. This covenant was different, and it wasn't designed to include everyone on earth. This covenant was made strictly with the people of Israel, the direct descendants of Abraham.

When they left Egypt, they were just a large, loose family of freed slaves. But the Lord had a fantastic plan to transform them into an actual nation of people founded by God himself. His method of operation would begin as it always does when he deals with humans: offer a covenant.

This covenant is the only works-based covenant God ever initiated with humanity. It was an "if, then" covenant. It was conditional. It was provisional. There were incredible blessings . . . or tragic curses for the generation of Israelites that broke it. Unfortunately, the weight of the curses eventually collapsed on Israel to the point of no return, and Israel ceased to exist as a nation of sovereign people around 586 BC. They were ruled by foreign kings afterward, beginning with Nebuchadnezzar of Babylon. By

AD 70, the people of Israel were carted off into exile or scattered in fear to the ends of the earth.

A Womb for the Messiah

The "if" word first appears in Exodus 19 during God's initial offer to the people of Israel. "Now if you obey me fully and keep my covenant, then out of all nations you will be my treasured possession. Although the whole earth is mine, you will be for me a kingdom of priests and a holy nation" (vv. 5-6a). We are already on new ground. God had never said "if" with Noah or Abraham. He technically never said "if" to Adam either. He just told Adam what would happen should fruit from the forbidden tree be eaten.

What was God saying here? What was he up to? These children of Abraham (with whom he was still in covenant on a different level) were now being offered a second covenant that would specifically establish them as a national entity, a country founded and led by God's own Spirit. They were to be a "kingdom of priests." God was to be their King, and they were to be priests, or intermediaries, who could stand before God on behalf of others. They were to be the point of intercession through which God would introduce the world's Messiah (as a fulfillment of the Abrahamic covenant).

Furthermore, the Israelites were told they would no longer be just a large family with various tribes comprising their company. They would become an actual nation, a holy or "set apart" nation. They had a destiny, a divine purpose to play for God. They were to teach the world about the necessity of performing and trusting in blood sacrifice for the forgiveness of sin in order to be righteous before God. Additionally, they were to be a safe place for the Messiah, the very Lamb of God, to one day be born.

Moses passes the offer down to the elders. They quickly and gladly accept! Why not? They had just experienced four major miracles! He had delivered them out of slavery. He had fed them manna and quail. He had sent water from a rock. And he had supernaturally destroyed the threat of the Amalekites. This God of Abraham was phenomenal and worthy of their honor.

The Spectacle on Mount Sinai

Shortly after, the day arrived. Some scholars believe between one and two million people gathered around the base of Mount Sinai for the covenant to commence. Billowing smoke, thunder-claps, lightning, even the sound of a heavenly trumpet—all emanate from the top of the mountain. But perhaps what was most striking of all, and something we often overlook, is that a large number of people together at one time audibly heard the voice of God in their own Hebrew tongue!

He voiced what we call the Ten Commandments in Exodus 20. The "thou shalt nots."

Can you imagine the scene? No wonder it scared the daylights out of them. They backed down, telling Moses they were too scared to be priests before this awesome God. But in those early moments, they missed the point of God's manifest display of power. It was only to "impress on" them the absolute reverence of God so they would not sin against the covenant they were about the cut!

The mob asked Moses to go up and be their covenant representative. Moses relented. The remainder of the Law (Exod. 20:22—23:33) was given in private to Moses. It is noteworthy to observe the final words of God in 23:32-33, when referring to people they were to drive out of the land: "Do not make a covenant with them or with their gods. Do not let them live in your land or they will cause you to sin against me, because the worship of their gods will certainly be a snare to you."

The Lord was imploring his people to remain utterly faithful to this covenant. He was also implying that they would be tempted to enter into other covenants that would be in direct contradiction to the Sinaitic covenant they were now entering.

The pull of the world can have the same effect on us today. God clears a new path for us to walk in through the new covenant in Christ and gives us strength to overcome our spiritual enemies. But then later we are prone to easily fall prey to the temptations of the flesh surrounding us.

In Exodus 24, Moses returned and told the people about the rest of what God had said and the laws he had uttered. The people said, "Everything the LORD has said we will do" (v. 3). The stage is now set. An altar is erected. Animals are slain. Blood is put in bowls and sprinkled on both the altar and a handful of people representing the three million Israelites watching. Sounds like a scene from a horror flick! Only this blood was spilled in the passion of covenant commitment, not cold-blooded murder.

Moses and the elders join God on the mountain, and another amazing event happens. They actually "saw the God of Israel . . . they saw God, and they ate and drank" (vv. 10a, 11b). What does this sound like? The covenant meal of the Sinaitic covenant!

It is shortly after this meal that Moses is called up to Mount Sinai. He will be gone forty days. Moses receives a "hard copy" of the words of the Ten Commandments: the initial terms of which we know today as the Sinaitic covenant or the old covenant.

Why Two Tablets?

Why did Moses return with a pair of stones? Many a Sunday school lesson plan has taught and illustrated that the first five commandments were inscribed on one table and the second five commandments were written on the second one. Does this mean God's handwriting was too big for all Ten Commandments to fit on one tablet? Of course not!

Was God just trying to give the already aging Moses a good physical workout on his way down the mountain? *You need to get in shape, pal; I'm going to double your payload. Better stretch your back before you start back down.* Highly unlikely.

So the question remains: why two tablets? The reason is found through the filter of covenant knowledge. When covenants were cut in ancient Bible times, each party was given a copy of the covenant terms (obligations, rules, etc.).

Covenant historian Meredith Cline notes in *The Correlation of the Concepts of Canon and Covenant* this common method. "Moreover, copies of the text, duplicates of which were prepared for all the parties concerned, were to be preserved in the presence of a god, carefully guarded, and periodically read publicly in the vassal kingdom."[1]

God was simply giving one full copy of the Ten Commandments to Moses and one to himself. He later instructed Moses to put both tablets inside the ark of the covenant (hence the term "covenant") because God was not going to take his tablet and return back to the sky with it. He was essentially saying, "You go ahead and keep my copy, Moses, because I'm going to live with you and the rest of Israel." God planned on inhabiting himself with Israel in the holy of holies where the ark of the covenant would be located!

The first set of tablets, which Moses destroyed in anger at the sight of the rebellious Israelites, was "the work of God" (Exod. 32:16). He literally fashioned them out of the mountainside. But the second set of tablets was different. This time the Lord told Moses to do the work. "Chisel out two stone tablets like the first ones, and I will write on them the words that were on the first tablets, which you broke" (Exod. 34:1). In this manner God was saying he placed much value on Moses as the covenant representative. It is an honor in covenant making to be chosen to prepare the blank sheet (or in this case, the blank Sheetrock!) on which the terms will be written.

Negative Is Positive

On the surface, the giving of the Ten Commandments is very negative. Eight out of ten are prefaced with "You shall not" orders.

Why such negativity? Isn't this supposed to be a joyous covenant ceremony full of positive thinking and encouragement? Before we label God a holy grouch, we must remember the state of humankind and how far humanity has traveled in time away from the sinless garden of Eden. We must remember that humans are now naturally opposed to God and therefore, when left to themselves, will do everything opposite to good common sense and morality. We don't need to teach our children how to lie or steal, do we? It comes quite naturally.

But we still love our children, and God still loves that part of creation made in his image. So both parents and the Parent of humanity train their children through warnings and negative reinforcements to teach the difference between right and wrong.

"Don't touch that stove, Joey!"

"Don't be stingy with your toys, Susie!"

"Don't run in the grocery store, Michael!"

"Don't pull your sister's hair, Billy!"

Not too different from God saying "you shall not" to the children of Israel, right? But as a child matures into young adulthood, the conversation slowly changes to heart-to-heart discussions and logical reasoning about the wisdom of God in any given situation. God did the same thing with the Sinaitic covenant. He has a grand master plan at work, and we cannot just pull a few chapters out of Exodus and say, "You see, God is such a killjoy and restrictive deity."

He was actually providing them with more than a moral code in this covenant. It was God's holy test-tube experiment on how a nation fully devoted to him should live and operate together. He gave them incredibly practical information about proper waste management, healthy eating habits, and medical examinations. His instructions included teaching Israel on many societal fronts: regulating justice, establishing cities of refuge, marriage arrangements, the cycle of festivals, the tithe and year of jubilee, rights of the firstborn, and driving out the nations around them. And he was extremely detailed about the proper method of making blood sacrifices and their purpose.

Blood and Sin

This Sinaitic covenant was by far the bloodiest covenant ever made in the Bible. Under this covenant over the centuries, thousands upon thousands of animals died as sacrifices. This constant bloodshed answers the two primary reasons why God cut this covenant to begin with.

The first reason was to reveal humanity's guilt and the deceitfulness of sin. Romans 7:7-12 says:

What shall we say, then? Is the law sinful? Certainly not! Nevertheless, I would not have known what sin was had it not been for the law. For I would not have known what coveting really was if the law had not said, "You shall not covet." But sin, seizing the opportunity afforded by the commandment, produced in me every kind of coveting. For apart from the law, sin was dead. Once I was alive apart from the law; but when the commandment came, sin sprang to life and I died. I found that the very commandment that was intended to bring life actually brought death. For sin, seizing the opportunity afforded by the commandment, deceived me, and through the commandment put me to death. So then, the law is holy, and the commandment is holy, righteous and good.

The Israelites still sinned under the Abrahamic covenant. They didn't see their need of the Abrahamic covenant because they didn't realize the extent of their sin! So God gave another covenant, the covenant of Law at Mount Sinai, to show them how desperately they needed the grace of the Abrahamic covenant. The Law comes that sin "might abound" (5:20, NKJV). It stirs up the deceitfulness of sin inside us. The Law is like the red cloak to a bull! "Come on, you want to see how bad you are! Come on and try to get me!"

The second reason was to place Israel under a schoolmaster until Christ came. Galatians 3:23-25 says, "Before the coming of this faith, we were held in custody under the law, locked up until the faith that was to come would be revealed. So the law was our guardian until Christ came that we might be justified by faith. Now that this faith has come, we are no longer under a guardian."

For centuries, God instructed Israel on what basis humans can approach him. "Find a lamb. Examine the lamb. Select a spotless lamb. Let's sacrifice this unblemished lamb. Without the shedding of blood there is no forgiveness. The lamb dies instead of you." This is repeated over and over until ingrained in the psyche of the Israelite. The only way to God is a blood sacrifice substitute! He was priming their pump to receive the revelation of the Lamb of God that would take away the sin of the world!

The key verse in the entire Torah is found in Leviticus 17:11: "It is the blood that makes atonement for one's life." The writer of Hebrews gave additional commentary on this Levitical verse in 9:22: "In fact, the law requires that nearly everything be cleansed with blood, and without the shedding of blood there is no forgiveness."

A Startling Discovery

In 1954, Researcher G. E. Mendenhall was able to demonstrate that the Sinaitic covenant bore a remarkable similarity to the ancient Hittite treaty official documents. The Hittites were a tribe of pagan people living in the land of Canaan during the time of the ancient Israelites. These Hittite treaties were made between a Hittite sovereign (suzerain) and a conquered vassal.[2]

The evidence was the outline of the book of Deuteronomy. It perfectly matches an official covenant treaty's outline from the Hittite culture. In short, Deuteronomy is the written contract of the covenant. The four parts of a Hittite document were (1) preamble: the name of the greater lord (suzerain) is identified; (2) historical prologue: a reciting of the suzerain's previous engagement with the weaker ruler (vassal), typically including benevolent acts; (3) stipulations/terms: the obligations imposed by the suzerain upon the vassal are spelled out; and (4) sanctions: the blessings and curses of the covenant are recorded.

Note the amazing structure of the book of Deuteronomy:

1. **Preamble.** The name of the suzerain, the Lord God, is identified (1:1-8).

2. **Historical Prologue.** Reciting of God's history with Israel, including benevolent acts (1:9—4:49).

3. **Stipulations.** The Ten Commandments plus numerous other commands and rules given to Israel (5—26).

4. **Sanctions.** Blessings and curses pronounced by God over Israel through a massive stage play at Mount Ebal and Gerazim and also through his servant Moses (27—30).

The Bible has a wide variety of genre: history, poetry, worship songs, testimonies, doctrine, prophecy, and so forth. But Deuteronomy takes a very special place in the canon of Scripture containing sixty-six books. It is the only book specifically set aside as an official record of a covenant. As a comparison, Israelites in 2000 BC would revere Deuteronomy as Americans admire the US Constitution or the Declaration of Independence.

Summary of the Steps

To review, we can identify the following covenant steps in the Sinaitic covenant:

Representative: Moses was the primary representative for Israel, but several others joined him in the ceremony: Aaron, Nadab, Abihu, and seventy elders.

Term and Blessings/Curses: The terms are specifically laid out in much of Deuteronomy 5—26. The blessings promise prosperity and peace in the land promised to their forefather Abraham. We can also lean back into Exodus 19 when God promises them the blessing of being his treasured possession, a kingdom of priests and a holy nation.

However, Deuteronomy 29:23-26 gives a very specific set of curses that would happen to an apostate Israel. It is a chilling account of what was to come:

The whole land will be a burning waste of salt and sulfur—nothing planted, nothing sprouting, no vegetation growing on it. It will be like the destruction of Sodom and Gomorrah, Admah and Zeboyim, which the LORD overthrew in fierce anger. All the nations will ask: "Why has the LORD done this to this land? Why this fierce, burning anger?" And the answer will be: *"It is because this people abandoned the covenant of the LORD,* the God of their ancestors, the covenant he made with them when he brought them out of Egypt. They went off and worshiped other gods and bowed down to them, gods they did not know, gods he had not given them." (Emphasis added)

Blood Sacrifice: The animals from Exodus 24 can be defined as the initial blood sacrifice that established the covenant.

Seals: No specific seals were required for this covenant.

Oaths/Vows: In Exodus 24:7, the people are recorded as saying, "We will do everything the LORD has said; we will obey."

Exchanges: No specific exchanges are recorded in Scripture for this covenant.

Meal: This meal is found in Exodus 24:11 when Moses, Aaron, Nadab, Abihu, and seventy elders "saw God, and they ate and drank."

Memorials: Mount Gerizim and Mount Ebal are by far the most significant memorials of this covenant. These two mountains in the Promised Land served as the locations where half of the tribes shouted blessings of the Sinaitic covenant on Mount Gerizim and the other half of the tribes proclaimed the curses of the Sinaitic covenant.

It was a ceremony on the grandest of stages and was a constant reminder in the distant horizon for any Israelite to remember the covenant. In view of these mountains, many an Israelite in that first generation likely thought twice before disobeying the covenant!

The Weight of the Covenant Curses

But the shine soon wore off. The tragic story of Israel under this covenant is heartbreaking. Within weeks of the glorious covenant ceremony on Mount Sinai, cracks begin to form. They make a golden calf and name it Yahweh while Moses is still up on the mountain.

God gives them a second chance.

They eventually refuse to enter the land of Canaan at God's command. Korah leads a team of rebellious malcontents against Moses.

God shows frustration, yet relents.

A complaining spirit festers like a virus that can't be contained. They marry the foreign women of Moab against God's direct orders.

God warns them they will lose his blessing and covering.

Priests begin to ignore their holy calling, highlighted by Eli and his sons Phineas and Hophni. When Israel demands an earthly king, God gives them Saul, who gives Israel forty years of faithless leadership.

God's patience wears thin, but he continues to show mercy. He raises up David, who is given the revelation of this mercy.

Most of David's descendants fail to serve God and Israel with covenant fidelity, culminating in Zedekiah, who has the audacity to break a covenant of peace with the benevolent King Nebuchadnezzar. A summary of the national sins against the Sinaitic covenant are registered in 2 Kings 17:7-15.

After approximately nine hundred years, the nation collapses under the weight of the broken Sinaitic covenant. God says, "Enough!" and sends the prophet Jeremiah as the divorce attorney to the people of Israel. Jeremiah must announce the worst of all news. A covenant's curses are as powerful as its blessings; the Sinaitic covenant is now over. God is divorcing Israel. No wonder Jeremiah was called the Weeping Prophet. The word of the Lord he was sent to deliver broke his own heart. The book of Lamentations is his despondent commentary over Israel's lost status as a covenant nation with Yahweh.

Israel has learned that humankind can't play fast and loose with God and get away with it. God will not be mocked. It must be stressed that Israel was not just "grounded" or "put in time out." The Hebrew word Jeremiah used in 31:32 for "broke" means "to make null and void." Their constant disobedience had reached its fill. Israel was cast into exile. Never again was Israel a free people. They were under Babylonian, Persian, Roman, or Greek authority. Some Israelites even went back to Babylon, the original land of Abram in Ur of the Chaldees! They were back to square one.

8

WILL THE REAL OLD COVENANT PLEASE STAND UP?

We have just explored two very important covenants in the last two chapters: Abraham's covenant (also called Abrahamic) and Moses' covenant (also called Mosaic or Sinaitic). Both unfold within the pages of the Old Testament or old covenant section of the Bible. Besides these two, we also explored Adam's covenant, Noah's covenant, and David's covenant. All five are found in the Old Testament. So to which of these covenants does the term "old covenant" refer?

Most scholars agree that Adam, Noah, and David are not the reference for the old covenant. That leaves Abraham and Moses. This chapter will offer an explanation by comparing and contrasting these two different covenants. Let's start with reviewing the key differences. Several times in Deuteronomy, Moses differentiates between the Abrahamic and the Sinaitic covenants. He is making it clear to Israel that they connected to God via a pair of very distinctive covenants. One is unconditional and permanent. That's the Abrahamic. The Sinaitic, however, is conditional and therefore potentially temporal.

Deuteronomy Details

Listen to what God told Moses in Deuteronomy 4:23-31 shortly after he foretold that Israel in future generations would indeed break the Sinaitic covenant. It is a little lengthy but makes a very important point.

Be careful not to **forget the covenant of the LORD your God that he made with you**; do not make for yourselves an idol in the form of anything the LORD your God has forbidden. For the LORD your God is a consuming fire, a jealous God. After you have had children and grandchildren and have lived in the land a long time—if you then become corrupt and make any kind of idol, doing evil in the eyes of the LORD your God and arousing his anger, I call the heavens and the earth as witnesses against you this day that you will quickly perish from the land that you are crossing the Jordan to possess. You will not live there long but will certainly be destroyed. The LORD will scatter you among the peoples, and only a few of you will survive among the nations to which the LORD will drive you. There you will worship man-made gods of wood and stone, which cannot see or hear or eat or smell. But if from there you seek the LORD your God, you will find him if you seek him with all your heart and with all your soul. When you are in distress and all these things have happened to you, then in later days you will return to the LORD your God and obey him. For the LORD your God is a merciful God; **he will not abandon or destroy you or forget the covenant with your ancestors**, which he confirmed to them by oath. (Emphasis added throughout chapter)

This can be a puzzling verse since God says he will destroy them for breaking a covenant, yet moments later he says he will not destroy them because of a covenant. How does this verse make any sense? The answer is that he is referring to two different covenants. The first covenant referenced in bold is the Sinaitic covenant, which was made between God and the people in Moses' time. It would also include their descendants.

The second covenant referenced in bold is the Abrahamic covenant, which was made between God and the ancestors (or forefathers: Abraham, Isaac, and Jacob) of the people in Moses' time. The second covenant remains forever intact because it is an unconditional covenant that God made to Abraham and his descendants.

It is as if the people of the Sinaitic covenant had a back-up covenant to lean on for hope for the future should God's dream of a national covenant with Israel ever collapse on itself through disobedience.

We see the clear distinction again in Deuteronomy 5:2-3, "The LORD our God made a covenant with us at Horeb [Sinai]. It was not with our ancestors that the LORD made this covenant, but with us, with all of us who are alive here today." God distinguishes the Sinaitic (also called Horeb) covenant as a promise not made to their ancestors (Abraham, Isaac, Jacob).

In Deuteronomy 6:18-19 God reminds the Sinaitic covenant generation that if they obey this covenant, they will inherit the promises of the Abrahamic covenant: "Do what is right and good in the LORD's sight, so that it may go well with you and you may go in and take over the good land the LORD promised on oath to *your ancestors*, thrusting out all your enemies before you, as the LORD said."

He does it again in Deuteronomy 7:12: "If you pay attention to these laws and are careful to follow them, then the LORD your God will keep his covenant of love with you, as he swore to *your ancestors*."

Can you see the continual delineation between two covenants?

Toward the end of the book, God announces another revealing truth that confirms the perpetual nature of the Abrahamic covenant even though Israel may fall away. "The LORD will also bring on you every kind of sickness and disaster not recorded in this Book of the Law, until you are destroyed. You who were as numerous as the stars in the sky will be left but *few in number*, because you did not obey the LORD your God. Just as it pleased the Lord to make you prosper and increase in number, so it will please him to ruin and destroy you. You will be uprooted from the land you are entering to possess" (Deut. 28:61-63).

God will not utterly destroy and wipe out every single descendant of Abraham. There will be a remnant of Israelites left alive to carry out God's promise to Abraham. Though the national sovereignty of Israel will be at stake, a remnant will remain. God must preserve them because of his covenant oath to Abraham.

The Old Has Passed Away

Since the Abrahamic covenant is everlasting and points to the Messiah in the coming of Jesus Christ, it is never abolished. The Sinaitic covenant was abolished, therefore, it is termed the old covenant. In Hebrews it is sometimes also called the first covenant in the context of blood sacrifices before God.

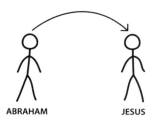

ABRAHAM   JESUS

The following passage in Hebrews 8:6-13 is lengthy but serves as one of the key texts for the difference between the old and first Sinaitic covenant and the new and better new covenant. Much of this passage is a reciting of Jeremiah 31:31-34.

But in fact the ministry Jesus has received is as superior to theirs as the covenant of which he is mediator is superior to the old one, since the new covenant is established on better promises. For if there had been nothing wrong with that first covenant, no place would have been sought for another. But God found fault with the people and said:

"The days are coming, declares the Lord,
 when I will make a new covenant
with the people of Israel
 and with the people of Judah.
It will not be like the covenant
 I made with their ancestors

when I took them by the hand
    to lead them out of Egypt,
because they did not remain faithful to my covenant,
    and I turned away from them,
                        declares the Lord.
This is the covenant I will establish with the people of Israel
    after that time, declares the Lord.
I will put my laws in their minds
    and write them on their hearts.
I will be their God,
    and they will be my people.
No longer will they teach their neighbor,
    or say to one another, 'Know the Lord,'
because they will all know me,
    from the least of them to the greatest.
For I will forgive their wickedness
    and will remember their sins no more."

By calling this covenant "new," he has made the first one obsolete; and what is obsolete and outdated will soon disappear.

These verses are loaded with important covenant references. We can quickly discern that the covenant made with Israel's ancestors when they left Egypt is the Sinaitic covenant. They failed to keep that covenant. So God will one day make a new "national" covenant. Jeremiah is told it will be made with the people of Israel and Judah. Humanity learns later through the words of Jesus and New Testament writers that this new covenant will also one day include all believing Gentiles.

In this new covenant, the members are called the people of God and the laws inside God's heart will be supernaturally deposited into the hearts of individuals instead of inscribed on stone tablets. All will "know" the Lord, which means to be intimately acquainted with. Wickedness will be forgiven. Sin will be remembered no more.

Thank God for the new covenant in the Lord Jesus Christ!

Hebrews continues to explain that Jesus actually took the curses of the broken Sinaitic covenant for Israel. He also took the curses of the broken Adamic covenant! Therefore, the word "first" in the following verse has a powerful double meaning. "For this reason Christ is the mediator of a new covenant, that those who are called may receive the promised eternal inheritance—now that he has died as a ransom to set them free from the sins committed under the first covenant" (Heb. 9:15).

"It Is Finished"

They are the three most important words Jesus ever uttered. When Jesus cried "It is finished" on the cross (John 19:30), he was making several statements. First, the administration of the curse of the Adamic covenant is over. A representative man has died by being separated from God for eating of the Tree of Knowledge of Good and Evil. Remember Jesus felt the presence of his Father leave him as he was dying: "My God, why have you forsaken me?" (Matt. 27:46).

Second, the power of the curse of the Sinaitic covenant is over. We see this from Hebrews 9:15 above. Two additional verses reference this fact. "Do not think that I have come to abolish the Law or the Prophets; I have not come to abolish them but to fulfill them" (Matt. 5:17).

In Ephesians 2:14-15, Paul writes, "For he is our peace; in his flesh he has made both groups into one and has broken down the dividing wall, that is, the hostility between us. He has abolished the law with its commandments and ordinances" (NRSV).

But you may ask, "Wait a minute. Why does Jesus say he would not abolish the Law and yet Paul says he abolished the Law in his flesh?" Seems to be a strange contradiction on a very important point. However, a closer examination of those words helps to clarify. The word "abolish" used by Jesus in the original Greek text is *kataluō*, which means "to dissolve, disunite, demolish, destroy."

The word "abolish" used by Paul in the Greek text is *luō*, a root of *kataluō* that means "to loosen or set free."

How can we make sense of these words when most of us don't speak Greek? One way is by understanding that Jesus did not plan on overthrowing the Law and the Ten Commandments of the Sinaitic covenant to make them irrelevant. Instead, he was going to obey them to the full and earn the right to reposition them: inside the desires of an individual's heart.

Paul said that when Jesus died and rose again, he abolished or "set free" from humanity the requirement to be right in God's sight by outwardly obeying the Ten Commandments and the remainder of the Law with all its necessary animal blood sacrifices.

But in the Scriptures between the Sinaitic covenant and the new covenant remains one more very important covenant. Its theme is about the perpetual reign of an earthly king and his descendants, culminating in the eternal establishment of the one true King from the line of David.

9

DAVID'S COVENANT

David had slain Goliath, then fled from Saul. And he had waited patiently for Samuel's prophetic word to come true: that one day a little shepherd boy would ascend to the throne of Israel.

In God's timing David became king. With the Abrahamic covenant in mind, he began to conquer lands, expand borders, and exert divine influence in the region. David had even returned the ark of the (Sinaitic) covenant from the home of Abinadab back to the City of David. He prepared a special tent for it to dwell with much joy and celebration. The ark of the covenant was now in Jerusalem.

David was clearly on a roll.

Let's pick up the story at this point beginning in 2 Samuel 7:1-3: "After the king was settled in his palace and the LORD had given him rest from all his enemies around him, he said to Nathan the prophet, 'Here I am, living in a house of cedar, while the ark of God remains in a tent.' Nathan replied to the king, 'Whatever you have in mind, go ahead and do it, for the LORD is with you.'"

David had begun to enjoy some of the good life of being king. He had a palace and surely a handful of servants and other niceties of royalty. Yet his heart was troubled, perhaps he even felt a little guilty. The ark of the covenant needed more honor than it was receiving. A tent? Really? God's ark needs its own house! David consulted Nathan the prophet, who agreed to what David's wishes were for the ark.

God's Play on Words

Later that same night, God spoke to Nathan and told him he had made a mistake. God explained that he had never required a house of cedar for his ark or complained about his living conditions among the people of Israel inside a tent (the old tabernacle). Perhaps with a twinkle in his eye and a touch of humor, the Lord then proceeds to lay out a play on words for David and Nathan. He begins by telling Nathan to tell David, "Are you the one to build me a house to dwell in?" (2 Sam. 7:5). God then recites how he had never complained about this before.

Several verses later God finally spits it out. "The LORD declares to you that the LORD himself will establish a house for you" (v. 11). This statement's irony in use of the word "house" cannot be overstated. Here was David trying to be nice to God by offering a new physical house for the ark of the covenant. Yet God responds with a word that David's line of descendants or "house" would be established. The word "house" in Hebrew means "genealogy or posterity."

What is happening here? God is saying that David has been chosen from all the thousands upon thousands of physical descendants of Abraham. He was to be the specific extension of the Abrahamic covenant. It's as if God is saying, "Remember when I told Abraham that through his seed all nations on earth will be blessed? Well, that seed is going to come through you, my servant David! You're the next point of reference. And I'm going to make this a covenant promise to you!"

The entire chapter of 2 Samuel 7 gives much detail to this covenant promise. And what makes it even more fascinating is that God uses the same pattern of an official covenant document of that era in speaking it! (Remember how the book of Deuteronomy is the official covenant document of the Sinaitic covenant? Second Samuel 7 is a condensed version of the same outline.) Here is the amazing breakdown.

1. **Preamble.** Where the name of the greater lord is identified, "This is what the LORD Almighty says . . ." (2 Sam. 7:8*a*).

2. **Historical Prologue.** The Lord reminds David of their shared history, "I took you from the pasture, from tending the flock, and appointed you ruler over my people Israel. I have been with you wherever you have gone, and I have cut off all your enemies from before you" (vv. 8*b*-9*a*).

3. **Terms.** An everlasting kingdom will be set up:

   Now I will make your name great, like the names of the greatest men on earth. And I will provide a place for my people Israel and will plant them so that they can have a home of their own and no longer be disturbed. Wicked people will not oppress them anymore, as they did at the beginning and have done ever since the time I appointed leaders over my people Israel. I will also give you rest from all your enemies. The LORD declares to you that the LORD himself will establish a house for you: When your days are over and you rest with your ancestors, I will raise up your offspring to succeed you, your own flesh and blood, and I will establish his kingdom. He is the one who will build a house for my Name, and I will establish the throne of his kingdom forever. (Vv. 9*b*-13)

4. **Sanctions.** The blessings and the curses, "I will be his father, and he will be my son. When he does wrong, I will punish him with a rod wielded by men, with floggings inflicted by human hands. But my love will never be taken away from him, as I took it away from Saul, whom I removed from before you. Your house and your kingdom will endure forever before me; your throne will be established forever'" (vv. 14-16).

There is much that can be mined out in these passages, but look closely at the key component that makes this covenant a direct link to Jesus Christ and the future new covenant. "He is the one who will build a house for my Name . . . I will be his father and he will be my son" (vv. 13*a*, 14*a*). God says that he is going to have his name attached to the covenant.

The Seed's Confusing Identity

A quick flyby of these verses can lead to some puzzling questions. God says the "seed" or offspring will build a house for him, and yet the seed will also need to be corrected. Can this seed strictly be the sinless Jesus Christ? Absolutely not—because a sinless, perfect Jesus needs no correction. This seed is referring to David's son Solomon.

Yet God also said the seed will have an everlasting kingdom. What we have here is a double prophecy unfolding in the Davidic covenant. It is clear the immediate physical "seed" is Solomon and his sons. They will be punished for their mistakes. The everlasting "Seed" is Jesus Christ, who will establish David's throne and God's kingdom forever.

We see a similar parallel to the Abrahamic covenant: the seed of Abram was Isaac, Jacob, twelve sons, but the Seed of Abraham is Jesus.

This is truly an astounding promise made to a human being by God. He is linking the line of David to his own eternal reign, and this covenant ultimately doesn't depend on David's descendants to keep it going.

The Covenant Set to Song

Psalm 89 offers a clear commentary on the Davidic covenant. The song was written by Ethan, who was likely one of David's choir leaders who lived well into the later reign of a king named Rehoboam (one of the sons of Solomon). He starts early by declaring what David learned in 2 Samuel 7. "You said, 'I have made a covenant with my chosen one, I have sworn to David my servant, I will establish your line forever and make your throne firm through all generations'" (Ps. 89:3-4).

These verses present a powerful teaching moment for the children of Israel and will serve to encourage them in darker years ahead. For the Christian today, it serves the same purpose as we await the ultimate coronation of Jesus Christ as the King over the City of David (Jerusalem).

Note that the songwriter Ethan later seems to pick up on what David had initially told him about this "kingdom covenant" on the earth and its unusual double prophecy. He seems to be writing lyrics for God to speak: "If his sons forsake my law and do not follow my statutes, if they violate my decrees and fail to keep my commands, I will punish their sin with the rod, their iniquity with flogging; but I will not take my love from him, nor will I ever betray my faithfulness. I will not violate my covenant or alter what my lips have uttered" (Ps. 89:30-34).

God is faithful to keep his covenant, even if his physical descendants stumble in their leadership. God emphasized it one last time through Ethan's lyrics in this chapter declaring that David's seed or "line will continue forever and his throne endure before me like the sun" (Ps. 89:36). This is obviously a reference to Jesus, who arrived on the scene about a thousand years later.

Mary and Joseph: A Match Made in Heaven

It was no coincidence that Joseph met Mary. Perhaps of all the marriages in the history of the world, this supposedly scandalous union was loaded with prophetic weight. Consider the following: David had nineteen sons. God had declared the kingdom would be given to Solomon's line. But Solomon had an evil son named Rehoboam who ruled over Israel (and later just the southern kingdom of Judah).

By the time King Ahab had infected the seed of David's line through illicit marriages, the writing was on the wall. Judgment was eventually placed on Solomon's line in Jeremiah 36:30-31, "Therefore, this is what the LORD says about Jehoiakim king of Judah: He will have no one to sit on the throne of David" (v. 30).

In other words, the line of Solomon was cut off! It was over for his family. Another one of David's sons would be chosen as the new line of royalty. Who would it be? The answer was kept hidden for centuries. It wasn't until the marriage of Joseph and Mary revealed Jesus as the final King on the throne of David.

How was this so? In Matthew 1 we see David's line begin with Solomon and continue to Joseph. But in Luke 3 we see David's line run from Nathan and continue to Mary! Both were direct descendants of David. Perhaps it is a bit of an irony that the new kingly line would come from David's son Nathan, the same name of the prophet who announced the Davidic covenant a thousand years earlier.

Matthew lists Joseph's father as a man named Jacob (Matt. 1:16). Yet Luke mentions that Joseph's father was a man named Heli, or Eli (Luke 3:23). Will the real father please stand up?

It should be noted that Jewish genealogies did not typically mention women in their lines. They were embedded in either their father or husband when necessary. Therefore, it would have been very normal to give the father-in-law the right of fatherhood in a genealogical listing. In Luke 1, it is apparent that Heli was actually the father of Mary and therefore, the father-in-law of Joseph.

Since Matthew and Luke clearly record much common material, it is certain that neither one could unknowingly incorporate such a flagrant apparent mistake as the wrong genealogy in his record. The two genealogies show that both parents were descendants of David. Joseph came through Solomon (Matt. 1:7-15), inheriting the legal right to the throne of David. Mary came through Nathan (Luke 3:23-31), carrying the seed of David.

Angels (and Prophets and Preachers) We Have Heard on High

The church has been putting on Christmas plays for centuries. Shepherds, angels, wise men, Mary, Joseph, and of course the baby Jesus. In 1996, my (Rob's) son Jenson was cast to be baby

Jesus for a CBN broadcast called *Alabaster's Song*. It was quite an experience to see him make his debut on the big screen just a few weeks old!

Although he didn't have any lines that day, the angel Gabriel near him did. They were not uncommon from many other Christmastime performances. "Do not be afraid, Mary; you have found favor with God. You will conceive and give birth to a son, and you are to call him Jesus" (Luke 1:30-31).

That's usually where the angel lines stop. But that's just half of what they are recorded as saying in Scripture. Listen to the last sentence that Gabriel spoke: "The Lord God will give him the throne of his father David, and he will reign over Jacob's descendants forever; his kingdom will never end" (vv. 32-33).

Gabriel was referencing the Davidic covenant and saying this covenant is about to be fulfilled in this child!

Later in the same chapter, Zechariah the father of John the Baptist prophesied in reference to the Davidic covenant as well. "He has raised up a horn of salvation for us in the house of his servant David (as he said though his holy prophets of long ago)" (Luke 1:69-70). A horn symbolizes strength in the Bible as Zechariah connects the birth of Jesus directly to the Davidic covenant.

This covenant was clearly on the minds of the angel Gabriel and sensitive followers of God in Israel during the time of Jesus' birth.

It was also prominent after his death and resurrection. In Acts 2:29-35 Peter stands up with boldness in front of his peers and shouts a mighty statement:

Fellow Israelites, I can tell you confidently that the patriarch David died and was buried, and his tomb is here to this day. But he was a prophet and knew that God had promised him on oath that he would place one of his descendants on his throne. Seeing what was to come, he spoke of the resurrection of the Messiah, that he was not abandoned to the realm of the dead, nor did his body see decay. God has raised this Jesus to life, and we are all witnesses of it. Exalted to the right hand of God, he has received from the Father the promised Holy Spirit and has poured out what you now see and hear. For David did not ascend to heaven, and yet he said,

"The Lord said to my Lord:

'Sit at my right hand

until I make your enemies

a footstool for your feet.'"

Peter stated that God raised Jesus back to life. A thousand years earlier, God told David, "I will raise up your offspring" (2 Sam. 7:12). Peter stated that Jesus was exalted to the right hand of God. The Lord told David, "I will establish the throne of his kingdom forever" (v. 13).

Let's walk backward in time and put all the covenant pieces together like the final act of a mystery theater performance.

- Fact 1: The Messiah of the new covenant had been born.
- Fact 2: The Davidic covenant had secured its final king to sit on the throne.
- Fact 3: The Abrahamic covenant had found the Seed that would truly bless the whole earth.
- Fact 4: The Adamic covenant had finally sprung forth the Offspring of Eve that would crush the head of Satan.

The clues all point to one person as the hinge of history hung in the balance. Jesus Christ had arrived as both the Son of Man and the Son of God on the earth!

In the next section we will dissect his covenant: the most powerful covenant of all ever made between God and humankind.

SECTION III
THE NEW COVENANT
BREAKS NEW GROUND

10

THE NEW COVENANT: HOW THE SOUL IS SAVED

Let's walk through the covenant-making ceremony again but from a new and *better* perspective. You see, the new covenant is better than the old covenant.

Look at Hebrews 7:22 and 8:6: "So much the more also Jesus has become the guarantee of a better covenant. . . . But now He has obtained a more excellent ministry, by as much as He is also the mediator of a better covenant, which has been enacted on better promises" (NASB).

In what way are the promises better? The answer to that is found in the word "atonement." We commonly use this word to describe what happened when Jesus died on the cross: he *atoned* for our sin. We find the term in the Old Testament over one hundred times. Surprisingly, in most translations of the *New* Testament the word "atonement" is not mentioned. The verb "atone" means "to cover." In the Old Testament sins were *covered*. But in the New Testament it is not a case of our sins being covered. What happens in the New Testament? Our sins are *wiped away*—they are *gone*! That's what the new covenant is all about.

There is another reason the promises of the new covenant make it superior to the old covenant. The old covenant is a *shadow* of the new covenant, which is "the real thing." Hebrews 10:1 says, "The law is only a shadow of the good things that are coming—not the realities themselves." By looking at a shadow, I can tell a lot about an object—what the real thing might look like. A shadow is only two-dimensional. My view becomes three-dimensional when I look at the object itself. And there is a great deal of difference between the two.

The Old Testament is a shadow of something yet to come. When we move to the New Testament, we are in a sense moving from two dimensions to three dimensions. In addition to that, Jesus is the incarnation, God coming in human flesh—the real thing. We see this concept clearly in the new covenant-making ceremony.

Observe now the powerful steps of the new covenant.

Representative

It is overstating the obvious that Jesus Christ is the representative of this covenant, and so we will not spend much time on this step. But it is fascinating to note what Isaiah prophesied about "the Servant of the LORD" (42:19) as a representative. "I will keep you and will make you to be a covenant for the people and a light for the Gentiles" (v. 6). Jesus is going to *be* a covenant, not just *cut* a covenant. This points directly to him as our covenant representative.

Paul picks up on this in Romans: "So then as through one transgression there resulted condemnation to all men, even so through one act of righteousness there resulted justification of life to all men. For as through the one man's disobedience the many were made sinners, even so through the obedience of the One the many will be made righteous" (5:18-19, NASB).

Jesus is seen here as the Last Adam (man). That is why the phrase "being born again" makes sense through the filter of covenant. We were all physically born under the covenant representative of the first Adam. That race is destined to die because of sin, which separates humankind from God.

The solution? We need to die to that race and be born again (under a different covenant) in order to live. When a person receives the glorious gospel of the new covenant, something amazing happens. He or she is "born again" (born a second time) under the covenant representative of the Last Adam.

Walk of Death

Although there is no specific mention of the actual step of the walk of death for Jesus, it is fascinating to note what happened after he was sentenced to die. He was given a cross to bear and forced to walk through the streets of Jerusalem (a type of "walk of death"). Once out of the city walls, he was led to the place called Golgotha where he was crucified.

Think about the significance of that "walk of death" and where it took place. As he walked, blood spilled from his body to the paving stones. Jesus was the representative walking in his own blood, since he was also to be the sacrifice of the new covenant. And it happened in Jerusalem, the City of God, the place on earth that the Lord esteems the most. Jesus lamented for the city and its residents just a day earlier. By the end of the death march, Jerusalem had been stained with the covenant blood of Jesus.

But look at its deeper purpose for us today. For we have a walk to take ourselves. The original purpose of the walk of death through the animal blood was to symbolize the loss of individual identity—effectively surrendering one's life. In the New Testament, Jesus says it this way: "You try to hang on to your life—you will lose it. You lay your life down for me—you will gain it. If you pick up your cross, you will follow me and you will die with me." Baptism reflects the same truth. When we go down into the water, we identify with his death. When we come out of the water, we identify with his resurrection to new life—his life.

The believer in Christ is required to take the "walk of death" by dying to self-centeredness and selfish ambition.

Blood Sacrifice

Earlier we talked about the heifer. In the new covenant it isn't a heifer that sheds its blood. Hebrews 10:19-20 says, "We have confidence to enter the holy place by the blood of Jesus, by a new and living way which He inaugurated for us through the veil" (NASB). Jesus, by choice, became the One who was slain in our covenant-making ceremony.[1]

Let's consider the historical crucifixion event. Matthew 27:50-51 depicts Jesus hanging on the cross just prior to dying: "Jesus cried out again with a loud voice, and yielded up His spirit. And behold, the veil of the temple was torn in two from top to bottom" (NASB). The veil divided what was called the holy place from the holy of holies. History suggests that the curtain—the veil—was very thick.

When Jesus died, the veil split[2] from top to bottom, recalling the imagery of slicing the heifer. The ripping also symbolizes the breaking of Jesus' flesh. It meant that believers were no longer separated from the holy of holies. There was no longer any need for a priest to mediate—the ultimate Mediator had come. Because the veil was ripped, we now have direct access to God. Jesus himself became the sacrifice—the pure, spotless Lamb of God.

It is the combination of the blood sacrifice and the representative who makes covenant noted earlier that makes the new covenant so astounding. They are the same person! Never had this happened before, and never will it happen again. In fact, the Hebrew word for "new" in Jeremiah 31 when the prophet describes this coming covenant means "unprecedented, unheard of, new in kind/nature."

Translation: *this covenant is going to astound you! It's the ultimate shock-and-awe campaign!* Before continuing to the next chapter, take a moment to ponder how God redeemed humankind through the distinctive nature of the new covenant.

The Mark on the Body

In the old covenant a mark was placed on the body—circumcision. In the New Testament we regard circumcision a matter of the *heart*. Romans 2:28-29 tells us, "A person is not a Jew who is one only outwardly, nor is circumcision merely outward and physical. No, a person is a Jew who is one inwardly; and circumcision is circumcision of the heart, by the Spirit, not by the written code. Such a person's praise is not from other people, but from God."

Paul says a person is not a Jew just by virtue of having the mark of circumcision on the physical body; the real Jew is one who is circumcised *inwardly*. The individual has made a conscious, deliberate choice and will not walk in the pathways of sinfulness any longer. Instead, the person will embrace righteousness.

Yet in full appreciation of the metaphorical allusion to circumcision of the heart as a seal/mark for believers, we can determine that Jesus bore a distinctive seal as the covenant representative. Isaiah 49:16 states, "See, I have engraved you on the palm of my hands." This unusual verse in the Old Testament can be explained in part as a picture of the nailed hands of Jesus on the cross. They became the covenant seal that made a clear distinction as to who was the representative of the new covenant. The prophet Isaiah was inspired again several chapters later to write a phrase about a piercing of the Messiah. "But he was pierced for our transgressions" (53:5).

Roman crucifixion of condemned men was not even invented until centuries later, yet God gave Israel ahead of time a clue to how the Messiah would make his mark (no pun intended!).

The Terms/Promises

The few words that Jesus spoke while in the process of cutting a covenant for us are among the most important in the entire Bible. These words were loaded with covenant terms. Among them are instructions (or terms) given to God the Father (the other partner of new covenant) to forgive people their sins! (Luke 23:34).

Remember Jesus had mentioned the forgiveness of sin while administering the elements of the Passover meal. Why did Jesus bring it up again on the cross? As he was flogged and crucified, every breath was painful enough, let alone every word spoken! The reason is that these specific words of forgiveness had to be spoken in those moments while the new covenant was being cut. They were the "terms or conditions." Forgiveness by God the Father was going to be a requirement on his part for any person who believed in the new covenant!

Jesus also took special words to comfort one of the two men crucified near him. He promised the criminal that he would join him in paradise later that day (Luke 23:43).

Exchange of Robes

Envision this: When Jesus and you entered into covenant, you both stood in an open field facing each other before a crowd of witnesses. In essence, Jesus said, "I'll exchange outer garments with you. I'll exchange robes." You look at your sport coat and then look at his. "Jesus," you say, "your coat is brand-new, top-of-the-line, the best I've ever seen. Mine is tattered and threadbare. I'm ready to throw it away."

"I know," he says. "I'll swap you even."

That's exactly what we did. We swapped outer garments. Our identities were confused, and consequently here's what happened: the Father took a long look at us and saw that we were each individually covered in robes of righteousness. "I like what I see," he said.

Then the Father looked down and saw his own Son, who was clothed in my robes of sinfulness. Jesus paid an extremely high price for swapping that outer garment. Second Corinthians 5:21 tells us, "He made Him who knew no sin to be sin on our behalf" (NASB).

The significance of the exchange of robes can also be seen in Philippians 2:7-8, "[He] emptied Himself, taking the form of a bond-servant, and being made in the likeness of men. Being found

in appearance as a man, He humbled Himself by becoming obe-
dient to the point of death, even death on a cross" (NASB). These
verses are called the *kenosis* passage. Translated from the Greek,
the concept is this: to empty oneself of oneself. You and I can't
do that, but God can and did. Jesus wrapped himself in my robe
of flesh, my robe of sinfulness. When the exchange of outer garments took place, I have, according to 2 Corinthians 5:21, "the
righteousness of God in [Christ]" (NASB). While everyone seems
so concerned about upward social mobility, Jesus chooses *down-
ward* social mobility in order to identify with us.

Exchange of Belts

When Jesus and I entered into covenant, we exchanged belts,
which represents the exchange of strengths. In 2 Corinthians
12:7-10 Paul wrote, "Because of the surpassing greatness of the
revelations, for this reason, to keep me from exalting myself, there
was given me a thorn in the flesh, a messenger of Satan to torment me—to keep me from exalting myself! Concerning this I
implored the Lord three times that it might leave me. And He has
said to me, 'My grace is sufficient for you, for power is perfected
in weakness.' Most gladly, therefore, I will rather boast about my
weaknesses." This is covenant language. Notice the exchange taking place—"that the power of Christ may dwell in me. Therefore
I am well content with weaknesses, with insults, with distresses,
with persecutions, with difficulties, for Christ's sake; for when
I am *weak*, then I am *strong*" (NASB, emphasis added). The exchange of belts symbolizes the exchange of strengths or assets.

The traditional interpretation of 2 Corinthians 12:7 is that
Paul's thorn in the flesh was a physical ailment, perhaps failing
eyesight. The most bizarre interpretation I have ever heard is that
it referred to his mother-in-law! I think there's a better interpretation. The term "thorn in the flesh" is a Hebrewism, an idiom
unique to the language. The phrase is used the same way we might
say "the four corners of the earth."

Of course, we don't believe the earth is flat and has corners, as people did centuries ago. We are speaking figuratively. We find similar phrases referring to a thorn three times in the Old Testament: Numbers 33:55; Joshua 23:13; and Judges 2:3 (see the NIV). In all three cases it refers to ungodly people trying to stop the work of God. I believe that is precisely what is referred to in 2 Corinthians 12:7. I propose that the thorn refers to ungodly (out-of-covenant) persons trying to block what God is doing through his covenant children.

According to 2 Corinthians 12, Paul cried out to God three times asking him to remove the thorn. He responded with a single phrase: "My grace is sufficient for you" (v. 9). Many persons have interpreted that to mean "Keep a stiff upper lip and hang in there, Paul. Just get through this one. It's going to be OK." But that's not what God is saying. I believe he's saying, "Paul, if anybody ought to know about grace, it's you. You've walked with me for years. You've proven me time and time again. You understand resurrection power. Operate in my strength."

For Christians, the standard interpretation of grace has generally been "unmerited love." That's not an inaccurate definition, but it is an inadequate definition. *Grace, biblically understood, is God's willingness to unleash his power in my behalf though I don't deserve it.*

This concept is intriguing. Nowhere does the New Testament ever say, "When Satan attacks you, cry out to God, who will get back with you as soon as he gets time."

It's not as if we call God on his hotline with no results: "Hello, God. Yeah, Satan's on my back again. How soon can you be here? Fifteen minutes? OK. I'll just hang in there in the meantime."

On the contrary, the New Testament tells us to live with power and authority, "[You] resist the devil, and he will flee from you," says James 4:7. The firepower of the enemy is no match for a believer armed with covenant authority. We can bring down the strongholds of the devil. Our weapons are mighty. Believers have power because God is willing to unleash his power on our behalf.

Zechariah 4 deals with this same truth. The Jewish people were assigned the task of rebuilding the temple after it had been destroyed by invading armies, and Zerubbabel was their leader. To rebuild the temple, the Israelites had to quarry rocks out of a great mountain.

In the midst of this seemingly impossible task, the word of the Lord came to Zerubbabel saying, "Not by might nor by power, but by my Spirit" (v. 6). Verse 7 continues, "What are you, O great mountain? Before Zerubbabel you will become a plain; and he will bring forth the top stone with shouts of 'Grace, grace to it!'" (NASB).

God is telling Zerubbabel to "speak grace" to a mountain. What does that mean? It means he's going to partner with you. "Together we'll bring this mountain down and make it a plain," God says.

In the New Testament we see mountains referred to again, this time as a Hebrew idiom. When Jesus tells us to "say to this mountain, 'Be taken up and cast into the sea'" (Matt. 21:21, NASB), he isn't referring to a literal mountain. All of us have mountains or difficulties we face in life, challenges and struggles. God is in the business of helping us bring down mountains and make them into plains.

What mountains are you facing in your life? God is willing to unleash his power in your behalf (that's grace) to bring them down. This is the exchange of strengths.

Exchange of Weapons

When Jesus and I entered into covenant, we exchanged weapons. This represents the exchange of enemies. I took on Jesus' enemy—Satan. He took on my enemy—death.

Death is the number-one enemy of humanity. We know that we cannot compete with death. It is coming to each one of us. But Jesus defeated our enemy. And because of what Jesus did, we can say, "O death, where is thy sting? O grave, where is thy victory?" (1 Cor. 15:55, KJV).

In Genesis 3:15 God speaks to Lucifer, saying, "There is enmity (strife) between you and Me" (author's paraphrase). Satan is God's enemy. Let's see how God has provided for the exchange of weapons so we can overcome his enemy. Paul writes in Ephesians 6:10, "Be strong in the Lord and in the strength of *His* might" (NASB, emphasis added). Here is the exchange of strength. The covenant language continues in verse 11: "Put on the full armor of God [*His* armor], so that you will be able to stand firm against the schemes of the devil" (NASB).

Apparently *we* are the ones who are supposed to take on the devil. "For our struggle is not against flesh and blood" (v. 12). Not the people who irritate us or bug us. Not the spouses who may have walked away. Not the kids who may have been rebellious. Not the bosses who may have fired us. Not with radical secularists who are blatantly anti-Christian. Our struggles, Paul continues, are "against the rulers, against the powers, against the world forces of this darkness, against the spiritual forces of wickedness in the heavenly places." In other words, the devil and the demonic kingdom. "Therefore, take up the full armor of God [note: *His* armor, thus an exchange], so that you will be able to resist in the evil day, and having done everything, to stand firm. Stand firm therefore, HAVING GIRDED YOUR LOINS WITH TRUTH, and HAVING PUT ON THE BREASTPLATE OF RIGHTEOUSNESS, and having shod YOUR FEET WITH THE PREPARATION OF THE GOSPEL OF PEACE; in addition to all, taking up the shield of faith

with which you will be able to extinguish all the flaming arrows of the evil one" (vv. 12-16, NASB).

This is the exchange of weapons, symbolizing the exchange of enemies. This is amazing. Christ took our enemy (death). We are to be equipped to challenge his enemy (Satan) on this earth.

Exchange of Names

Did you know that you will be given a new name by the Lord Jesus himself? When he addressed the church in Pergamum in the book of Revelation, the last thing he said to them referenced a covenant element: the giving of a different name. "To the one who is victorious, I will give some of the hidden manna. I will also give that person a white stone with a *new name* written on it, known only to the one who receives it" (2:17, emphasis added).

What an intimate moment Jesus has waiting in the wings! There is a secret name he has selected just for you, birthed from the deep friendship of his covenant with you. And it is to be written on a white stone, which symbolizes a declaration of innocence.

The ancient Greeks would vote on court cases by using black and white stones. Whenever a judge was about to issue his verdict against an accused man, he would reveal in his hand either a black stone or a white stone. A  black stone meant the person was guilty as charged. A white stone meant the person was deemed innocent and free from any further charges. It's also interesting to note the word for "vote" in modern Greek is close to the Greek word *psēphos* used in Revelation for stone. Jesus is issuing his believers an eternal "yes" verdict as we put our saving faith in his covenant blood.

We take on Christ's name in the term "Christ-ian" while Jesus takes on humanity's name in the term "Son of Man."

The Meal

An entire separate chapter will be devoted to the covenant meal of the new covenant. The first new covenant meal was simultaneously the last Passover meal that God intended. Jesus fulfilled the Passover meal's final purpose in his death the next day.

Yet this meal with his disciples is not the true covenant meal of the new covenant. Otherwise, the new covenant is just for twelve men in the entire history of the world! The Bible alludes to another amazing meal in Revelation 19:9, "Blessed are those who are invited to the wedding supper of the Lamb!" This supper shall be the true fulfillment of the new covenant. We even see a reference to us being married to Christ as a bride is married to the groom.

Jesus told his disciples that the meal he was sharing with them in that moment was really just a foretaste anyway. "I will not drink again from the fruit of the vine until the kingdom of God comes" (Luke 22:18). Our resurrected physical bodies will one day actually eat and drink with Jesus at the most amazing meal we will ever experience!

The Ministry of Reconciliation

Marshall McLuhan was a famous media theorist in the 1960s and 1970s. His most well-known phrase was "the medium is the message." McLuhan's insight was that a medium affects the society in which it plays a role, not by the content delivered over the medium, but by the characteristics of the medium itself.[3]

The apostle Paul probably would have agreed with McLuhan to some extent. While the content or raw "message" of the gospel could appear supernaturally as words in the clouds, it has never happened before in recorded history. And it likely never will.

In all practical terms, Paul reminded the early church that the gospel of the new covenant needs a human "medium" through which to communicate it. In 2 Corinthians 3:6 he says, "He has made us competent as ministers of a new covenant." Later in 2 Corinthians 5:19-20 he adds a word to describe the new covenant message. "And he has committed to us the message of reconciliation. We are therefore Christ's ambassadors, as though God were making his appeal through us."

The new covenant is the ultimate reconciliation appeal! "Come now, and let us reason together," the Holy Spirit cries out through the revelation of the new covenant, "though your sins are like scarlet, they will be as white as snow; though they are red as crimson, they shall be like wool" (Isa. 1:18, NASB).

The blessings of the new covenant are beyond imagination. They are the dream of God to bestow on his covenant children. But covenants don't just come with blessings. They also have curses attached for those who dare to break the covenant terms. And while his mercies are new every morning, it is possible for a person to enter the new covenant and then willingly choose to leave it behind. When that happens, there is no sacrifice for sin left and such a person is then truly and eternally lost.

The next chapter explores both the tremendous blessing and the tragic curse of the new covenant.

11

THE NEW COVENANT:
THE BLESSING AND THE CURSE CAUTION

Since Jesus is the embodiment of the new covenant, one would assume he would teach on covenant at every turn in his three-year public ministry. Isaiah prophesied that he would "be a covenant for the people" (Isa. 42:6). Jesus knew he was going to be both the representative and the sacrifice of God's new covenant, yet he was tight lipped on overusing the term "covenant."

In fact, he is not recorded even using the word "covenant" until the night of his betrayal. All the Synoptic Gospels (Matthew, Mark, and Luke) note the occasion. Luke's version reads, "In the same way, after the supper he took the cup, saying, 'This cup is the new covenant in my blood, which is poured out for you'" (Luke 22:20).

Why was he so quiet about discussing covenant until the end of his earthly life? It is difficult to determine the exact reason. Perhaps Jesus viewed the revelation of covenant much like he viewed the wisdom hidden inside his parables: it required someone "with ears to hear" in order to receive it.

Here Jesus unveils the reason behind the Hebraic covenant meal ritual (of eating bread and drinking fruit of the vine). The centuries-long foreshadow has found fulfillment in the giving of his own body (bread) and human blood (fruit of the vine). This moment is of such importance that he only shares this covenant revelation with his closest friends. Jesus' actions match what the Spirit of God revealed to David in Psalm 25:14. The Amplified Bible seems to fit best here: "The secret [of the sweet, satisfying companionship] of the Lord have they who fear (revere and worship) Him, and He will show them His covenant and reveal to them its [deep, inner] meaning."

They say a dying man's final words carry much weight. They are often the words most remembered. We mentioned some of these words in the prior chapter. But let's now examine his very last sentence.

As he hangs limp on the cross, Jesus is about to give up his Spirit. His voice rings out to the heavens: "It is finished!"

The silence must have lasted just a moment as he gave up his spirit. Suddenly, an earthquake! Rocks split. The temple curtain is ripped in half, and some of the dead rise out of their tombs. Whoa! What just happened? The "it" was "finished" in the death of Jesus! The "it" was the cutting of the new covenant!

But there is more. That cry from the lungs of Jesus was also the announcement concerning the curses of the broken Adamic covenant. The death sentence looming over the human race since the sin in the garden of Eden was being "fulfilled" or "executed" as Christ bore the sin of humankind on the cross. In this sense, the Adamic covenant was now "finished."

The Code Words of Jesus Reveal the Blessing

But let's take a step back into those three years again and take one more look at Jesus' words in the Gospels. Though he doesn't actually use the word "covenant," are there any allusions or illustrations to covenant? Phrases he used in parables? Prayers? Private discussions? It doesn't take long using our covenant filter to see Jesus teaching on the realities of living in a covenant relationship with him. The most obvious is John 15 in the account of the Vine and the branches.

Experience the covenant language, specifically the key preposition "in" as you read the following phrases pulled from his teaching.

"Remain *in* me, as I also remain *in* you" (John 15:4*a*).

"No branch can bear fruit by itself; it must remain *in* the vine" (v. 4*b*).

"*Apart* from me you can do nothing" (v. 5*b*).

"I have told you this so that my joy may be *in* you and that your joy may be complete" (v. 11).

Jesus uses this analogy to describe our covenant relationship with him because in the natural world a vine branch has no practical function other than to bear fruit for the vine. It cannot be used to start a fire or build a house. It is completely dependent on the life sap of the vine to give it identity, purpose, and destiny.

Blessings but No Curses

Do you remember that one of the steps in the covenant-making ceremony was the pronouncement of the blessings and curses? In the New Testament the blessings are found in Philippians 4:19—"My God will meet all your needs according to the riches of his glory in Christ Jesus." The blessings are reiterated in Romans 8:17, "[You are] heirs of God." What an amazing truth—*we are beneficiaries of everything he has!* In terms of the blessings of God, the resources of heaven have been released through Jesus to you because you are a joint heir with him.

And the curses? In the New Testament we don't find the pronouncements of curses. This is the only step of the covenant ceremony that is not paralleled in the New Testament. Why?

For years I (Jim) struggled to understand why the curses were missing. An experience in 1993 helped me make sense of my questions. When I lived in the Dallas/Fort Worth area, I joined other Christians on Saturday mornings at abortion clinics to pray for and offer help to young women considering that option, in hopes that they would choose against it. Many Christians attended, some with the organization Operation Rescue. These people often laid their bodies down in front of the door and blocked the entrance. Sometimes they were arrested for their passive protests.

As I observed the Operation Rescue volunteers, I discovered they were not a bunch of crazy fanatics, the way the media often portrayed them. They were just grandmas and grandpas, moms and dads, and teenagers. They were just normal church people who were so grieved by the thought of abortion that they literally laid their bodies in front of the clinic doors in hopes of saving lives. Every Saturday they would save at least one or two babies by their actions.

As I watched the Dallas police arrest Operation Rescue volunteers week after week, I became concerned about the officers' use of force. I contacted City Hall and raised my concerns to the office of the mayor of Dallas. As a result, Operation Rescue leaders asked me to act as a liaison between Operation Rescue and the Dallas police at these events.

In my role, I was to meet with the captain of the tactical unit and some of his key officers about three days before each rescue event took place. At one particular meeting, I was trying to persuade the police department to stop using a pressure point hold in which an officer would jam his thumb into the protestor's neck. The hold inflicted great pain, which forced an uncooperative person to walk. "You don't need to use this hold on these people," I said. "They are completely passive." My objections seemed to fall on deaf ears, and the tactics continued. Meeting after meeting I objected.

Finally in one meeting, Dan, the tall, single, quiet leader of Operation Rescue, who was being arrested every Saturday, interrupted my dialogue with the policemen.

"Let me tell you something," he said quietly. "You don't understand. We are *not* protestors. You may know how to handle union protestors or Ku Klux Klan protestors or gay rights protestors. But we are *not* protestors. What we are doing is an act of repentance."

Dan looked at the police officers. "We are not blaming the abortionists. We are not blaming you police officers. We are not blaming the politicians who gave us these laws. We are not blaming the young women who are pregnant, nor those who impregnated them.

"We think the blame is on *us*—the church of Jesus Christ who have been completely silent. *We are the problem.* You people are not supposed to stand for righteousness, but the church of Jesus Christ is. This is an *act of repentance* for our sin of silence.

"You can use the pressure point on me," Dan said. "You can do whatever you want. I don't care if you tear me limb from limb. I'm not looking for protection.

"I don't care if this Saturday you kill me. *Somewhere, somebody has to take the sin, the sickness, and the anger of this world and not pass it on.*"

When Dan said this to the policemen, I suddenly made the connection. I thought about an illustration I had heard in which upper management took their frustration out on middle management, who took it out on lower management. Then Dad (lower management) went home and yelled at Mom, who scolded Junior. Junior hit his little sister, who kicked the dog, who bit the cat. The cycle never stopped. The anger simply continued being passed on.

Dan said it again. "*Someone has to absorb the sin and the pain and not pass it on.* We'll take full responsibility for the sin of abortion in this nation."

With those words, I suddenly understood what had puzzled me for more than a decade. I now knew why there was no pronouncement of curses in the New Testament. You see, Jesus became the "Grand Shock Absorber," taking on the curses, fury, sickness, and sins of the ages. He absorbed the sin and the pain, and he didn't pass it on. That's why Galatians 3:13 says, "Cursed is everyone who hangs on a tree." In other words, Jesus "filters out" the horrible curses so that the blessings can come through. The next verse states "that the blessing given to Abraham might come . . . through Christ Jesus" (v. 14). So instead of "cursed are you," the New Testament knows only "blessed are you." The pronounce-ment of blessings and curses becomes, in the New Testament, the *absorption of curses* by Jesus and the *pronouncement of blessings* on all of us. We are free from the curse of sin!

But despite the absence of a direct curse in the new covenant, there yet remains the possibility that a person can effectively pass judgment upon himself or herself through raw arrogance and dis-respect. The ultimate illustration of this truth is seen by looking at a familiar Sunday school story between Israel and Egypt.

The Callous Heart of Pharaoh Reveals the Caution

What was Pharaoh thinking? He would dare to charge his troops into those walls of red water? It was clear God was on the side of Moses. Pharaoh didn't have a fighting chance, but then his hardening heart seemed to take over his decision-making process. This frightening scene of an unnecessary slaughter is a snapshot from one of those classic Sunday school lessons many Christians can easily recite from childhood. At first glance there seems to be no covenant connection at all, but rather, just a case of supreme arrogance in the sight of God.

But one day this image flashed through my mind as I (Rob) was reading in Hebrews 10. My covenant filter of interpretation brought Pharaoh's madness to serve as a sobering metaphor of dis-honoring the new covenant. The verse in focus here is Hebrews 10:29, "How much more severely do you think someone deserves to be punished who has trampled the Son of God underfoot, who has treated as an unholy thing the blood of the covenant that sanc-tified them, and who has insulted the Spirit of grace?"

The phrase "trampled the Son of God underfoot" suddenly propelled my mind to think of a visual. The first thought that came to mind from the Bible was the "trampling feet" of Pha-raoh and his men into the Red Sea documented in Exodus 14. It dawned on me that they had no business being there. This terri-tory, carved out by two red walls, was sacred ground. Only the

Israelites were permitted to cross. The covenant God had come to deliver his covenant people, and he was making a big show of his covenant fidelity. God would re-create the scene of his covenant ceremony with Abram on a much grander scale.

In Genesis 15 we see God in the smoking pot and fire torch.

In Exodus 14 we see God in the pillar of cloud and pillar of fire.

In Genesis 15 we see God in these two forms walking through two bloody red walls of the covenant animal sacrifices.

In Exodus 14 we see God in these same grander forms leading and flanking his beloved covenant people as they now walk through two red walls of water.

This is nothing less than a covenant renewal taking place. Anyone outside of this covenant dare not take one step into this private and sacred land! Yet here we see Pharaoh running headlong into quick judgment. He failed to treat this territory as holy. Pharaoh insulted the Spirit of grace, which initially was going to allow him to live if he would've just let God's people go!

What a similar fate then awaits those who do the same with the blood of the new covenant. When "we deliberately keep on sinning after we have received the knowledge of the truth" then all that is left is "a fearful expectation of judgment and of raging fire that will consume the enemies of God" (Hebrews 10:26-27).

Pharaoh provides the perfect symbolic picture of what happens to the person who hears the truth of the covenant gospel but then later turns his or her heart to sin and so despises it. Although the new covenant never directly mentions a curse, we see here a very sobering caution for anyone who would enter the new covenant, then deliberately choose to trample on its grace.

12

THE EVERLASTING COVENANT: THE ULTIMATE PURPOSE OF THE NEW COVENANT

Have you ever noticed there are a handful of New Testament verses that refer to something that happened before time began? We're talking before the universe was formed. Prior to anything in this physical realm. Earlier than Genesis 1:1.

What happened in advance of our time/space history that directly pertains to humankind? And why would it be mentioned in the Scriptures?

This chapter will make a strong suggestion that this "something" is the establishing and formation of a covenant within the Trinity himself. Between the Godhead of Father, Son, and Holy Spirit. The Bible calls this the everlasting covenant in the book of Hebrews, and it is by far the most fascinating and thought-provoking covenant ever made.

This covenant gives us clues to the very nature and essence of God himself. We are going to explore the possibility that God doesn't just make covenants, but that he *is* covenant. It is divine DNA. The everlasting covenant is not a typical sermon topic. But as you will see, it's one of the most important truths to grasp as a new covenant believer.

Because this covenant is somewhat mysterious, we need to think like a detective and create a character sketch. By piecing together several key scriptures, this is possible. The intention of this character sketch is not to present a random isogesis of the everlasting covenant. Isogesis is when someone "reads something into the Scriptures" to validate an argument about a particular topic matter. Rather, this chapter's focus is to merely expose you to the echoes and whispers of a covenant event that happened before time began. Our suggestion is that, like Mary after hearing from the angel about the coming birth of Christ, you treasure these things in your heart. Let the Holy Spirit give you final commentary on the truth of the everlasting covenant.

Character Sketch 1: Eternal

Scripture reveals five distinct features of the everlasting covenant. First, let's examine its obvious and self-evident trait: it is "eternal." Hebrews 13:20 says, "May the God of peace, who through the blood of the eternal covenant brought back from the dead our Lord Jesus . . ."

"Eternal" is also translated in Greek as "everlasting" or "outside of time." What is most unusual about this verse is that it speaks of blood! How can this be, since it happened outside of our time/space history? "Blood" here can also refer to life itself, so it seems that a life was given in order for this covenant to be established. Furthermore, this cryptic covenant suggests that it had the authority and power to resurrect Jesus Christ from the dead.

Character Sketch 2: Gift to Humanity

The second feature is that it contains a gift to humanity. Remember, the word "everlasting" means "outside of time." Second Timothy 1:9-10 says, "This grace was given us in Christ Jesus *before the beginning of time*, but it has now been revealed through the appearing of our Savior, Christ Jesus" (emphasis added). The key phrase that indicates this verse is talking about the everlasting covenant is obvious: *before the beginning of time!* Humankind was given grace "in Christ Jesus" (therefore via covenant) before we were created. Yet, we didn't know we had this grace available to us until the revealing of Jesus in our time/space history.

To illustrate this point, let's take something we all would love to receive as a gift: money. When my (Rob's) children do their chores around the house or mow the lawn, they earn money. In this day of online banking and ATM cards, my wife and I find it easier (and safer) to deposit their earned money directly into their individual checking accounts by transferring it from our primary checking account. However, this can sometimes be difficult for children to grasp. They like to see and feel the cold hard cash!

In order to obtain this pleasure and use it for shopping, they would have to go with us to a local ATM machine and make a withdrawal using their own debit card. When this happens, the deposit that was given to them before they go shopping is now being revealed in the physical world through the appearing of those bills spitting out of the ATM machine! The money was there, perhaps for weeks, but was not made visible until the time was right.

In the same way, this deposit of grace was eventually "cashed out" and "appeared" to humankind through the appearing of Jesus as the Son of Man in the earth. And humanity, those made in the image of God, are the only creatures who can understand and walk in this covenant because we are the only creatures to whom God made available this type of covenant love.

Character Sketch 3: Hidden from Angels

The third feature involves an intentional masking. It seems that God withheld the revelation of the everlasting covenant from the angelic host for a season. Ephesians 3:8-10 says, "This grace was given me . . . to make plain to everyone the administration [fellowship] of this mystery, which for ages past was kept hidden in God . . . through the church, the manifold wisdom of God should be made known to the rulers and authorities in the heavenly realms."

This fellowship within the Trinity's Godhead was kept hidden "for ages past," which seems to indicate a time period during our time/space history yet before the introduction of humankind in the earth. In other words, that strange gap that seems to be present between Genesis 1:1 and 1:2 when, among other events, Satan and a third of the angels rebelled against God.

Even today, the everlasting covenant and its connection to man appear to be a huge draw for the angelic. Peter says in reference to the salvation of humans, grace, sufferings, and glories that "even angels long to look into these things" (1 Pet. 1:12). Some angels do get a glimpse of the Trinity and are perpetually astounded. Right now as you read these words, "living creatures," which are a type of the angelic host, are crying out, "Holy, holy, holy is the Lord God Almighty, who was, and is, and is to come" (Rev. 4:8). The Bible says they never stop saying this phrase. They just repeat it over and over. Why?

It is possible they are continually mesmerized in sheer worship with unfolding fresh revelation about the love of God. Three times they cry "holy," which means "set apart or sacred." Why three? Holy is God the Father's love toward the Son. Holy is God the Son's love toward the Father. Holy is the Spirit's ability to include a creature—humankind—in this dance of love! Is "holy" said three times merely for emphasis, or could it be Trinitarian in its emphasis? This amazing possibility leads to the next feature of the everlasting covenant.

Character Sketch 4: Humans Were Chosen

The fourth trait is a specific selection: us! Ephesians 1:4 says, "For he chose us in him *before the creation of the world* to be holy and blameless in his sight" (emphasis added). Humankind is chosen to join this holy relationship within the Trinity. This has nothing to do with our performance before him. We did nothing to earn this right. Instead we were chosen out of all of God's glorious creations across the known universe to be "blood covenanted" to him.

And not only were we chosen for something special, but Jesus was chosen for something special. First Peter 1:19-20 says, "But with the precious blood of Christ, a lamb without blemish or defect. He was chosen *before the creation of the world*, but was revealed in these last times for your sake" (emphasis added). The Son, not the Father or the Spirit, was chosen in the deep counsel of the Godhead before the creation of the world to be the Lamb of the blood sacrifice of the everlasting covenant.

Character Sketch 5: A Promise Was Made

A covenant is no covenant without a promise to another. Titus 1:2 says, "God, who does not lie, promised *before the beginning of time*, and which now at his appointed season he has brought to light through the preaching" of his Word (emphasis added). The point of this verse brings to light yet again that something happened before time began: a promise was made. Now the presence of a promise indicates that at least two parties must be involved. You can't technically make a promise to yourself since you have no one externally to hold you accountable.

This fact is what makes the Trinity begin to make sense! Was this "promise before time began" made directly to us as human beings? No. We didn't exist yet! The promise of the everlasting covenant was made between the Father and the Son. And the One who oversees and mediates this covenant is the Spirit. As we have already begun to show, humankind was, in essence, included in the blessings of this covenant, but we were not partakers or even present when this covenant happened. In the same way Abraham was not present. He was sleeping during the pivotal moment of Genesis 15, during the covenant-making ceremony.

After these five brief character sketches, it is obvious God was up to something very significant before he "made the heavens and the earth." He was making a covenant. *An everlasting covenant.*

So what were the promises or terms of this covenant? Scripture seems to imply several of them that we will now examine.

God's Choice to Create Humans

Have you ever seriously pondered the question of why God chose to create humankind? Was he bored with himself. Bored with angels? Of course not. Just the opposite. Follow very carefully and consider the following statement: So glorious is the covenant love within his triune self that he willed to create other beings so like himself that they would be able to fully participate in the covenant life and love of the Trinity.

Wow!

Let's say it another way: *God desired to share himself outside of himself, and you are among those of his entire creation to whom God has specifically chosen to share his love with full knowledge and experience.*

Consider what possibly transpired in his mind as he contemplated the creation of the human race: "This covenant love we have within us is so utterly amazing that we must share ourselves with somebody else! We can't keep us to ourselves! Let us fashion a race of creatures capable of receiving and responding to our covenant love. They will be fearfully and wonderfully made. And each will be uniquely different and, therefore, have the opportunity to uniquely know a part of us."

And so he did. He made us in his image and in his likeness. We are so "like" God, yet we are not him at all. We are fearfully made, which means "to cause astonishment and awe." Think about that. When God made you, he was in awe of you! We are also wonderfully made, which means "distinguished and set apart." You are a one-of-a-kind creation.

God Purposed to Permit Sin

If humanity is to have the capacity to respond to the love inside the everlasting covenant, they must be given the capacity to reject it, or what we call a freewill choice. You cannot shower true love on a wooden puppet, for the puppet cannot freely reciprocate the love. A Pinocchio race is out of the question. What we have here is a very chilling prospect that must have given some pause within the Trinity: "We are considering the possibility of forming a creature that could reject our love and try to live independent of us. We must give the creature this choice to enter the dance of our love."

But the potential result in God's eyes that a creature could freely enter the fellowship of the mystery of his everlasting covenant love was so glorious, so marvelous, and so exciting that it was worth allowing a free will to come into existence who still might choose the horror of sin and death. Indeed, God knew humans would choose the horror of sin and death before he created them.

God has opened up his own type of catch-22 dilemma. If he chooses not to create humankind in order to avoid the potential rebellion, then the everlasting covenant is weaker than the possibility of sin!

If this is true, perhaps God was obligated to create a creature. This being would have both full knowledge and free will to validate God's own existence as covenant-maker and covenant-keeper. (Thus, the Tree of the Knowledge of Good and Evil would one day be present in the garden.)

So deep within the inner counsel of the Trinity before the creation of the universe, the Godhead asks the question of all questions: "What shall it cost us to bring this soon-to-be 'fallen man' out of his own sin?"

The verdict is clear: it shall cost the very lifeblood of God himself.

But in his astounding wisdom, God will choose to permit the possibility of sin while at the same time having the solution to completely deal with sin according to his holiness. The Trinity devises a way to extend mercy to sinful humankind without subverting his own justice.

Represent and Sacrifice

In order for the everlasting covenant to be released and extended to another with free will, it is determined that the Son of God will become the Son of Man (another reference to the name exchange of Jesus). He will come with a unique mission: to be both the covenant representative for humanity and the blood sacrifice for God.

"For this reason he [Jesus] had to be made like them, fully human in every way, in order that he might become a merciful and faithful high priest in service to God, and that he might make atonement for the sins of the people" (Heb. 2:17-18). This verse clearly speaks to Jesus the Son of God becoming also the Son of Man.

He will be "made like them, fully human in every way" and also become a "high priest." Both of these phrases directly address Jesus' role as a covenant representative or mediator. Jesus knew his role in the everlasting covenant would include having a physical body (Heb. 10:5).

Jesus also knew he would be the blood sacrifice of the everlasting covenant's offer to humankind. He knew what the Law of Moses (first five books of the Bible) taught about animal sacrifices under the Sinaitic covenant in Leviticus 17:11 and the powerful connections between blood, life, and atonement. "For the life of a creature is in the blood, and I have given it to you to make atonement for yourselves on the altar; it is the blood that makes atonement for one's life." He knew that verse was secretly pointing to himself as "the Lamb of God" who would one day take "away the sin of the world" (John 1:29).

The writer of Hebrews offers an even simpler version of this eternal truth: "Without the shedding of blood there is no forgiveness" (9:22). The sinless human blood of Jesus is the covenant blood of the everlasting covenant and was manifested to us as the new covenant at just the right time in God's providence.

SECTION IV
REMEMBERING A COVENANT

13

⸺

THE PLANTING OF A TREE:
A REMINDER OF THE COVENANT

In previous chapters we covered the steps of the covenant-making ceremony. An analysis of the ceremony in primitive cultures reveals that memorials, or reminders, were designed to prevent either party from forgetting the covenant. We'll mention two of them in this and the next chapter. Let's look at the first one—the planting of a tree.

The Place of the Oath

In Genesis 21:31-33 we read these words: "Therefore he called that place Beersheba, because there the two of them took an oath. So they made a covenant at Beersheba; and Abimelech and Phicol, the commander of his army, arose and re-  turned to the land of the Philistines. Abraham planted a tamarisk tree at Beersheba, and there he called on the name of the LORD, the Everlasting God" (NASB). This is an example of another step of the covenant-making ceremony, the planting of a tree. In this case it was a tamarisk tree, which is considered to be part of the palm family. In the Old Testament the palm is seen as the symbol of victory. Abraham and the Philistines entered into a covenant through the planting of the tree.

Personally, I (Jim) find this step a rather intriguing one. For many years I have given trees as gifts to very special friends. In elementary school my fifth grade teacher, Ethel Henthorne, gave me a crabapple tree. I planted it, and it grew from a tiny sapling to a very large tree. Every time I looked at it, I thought of that outstanding teacher. I was so excited about that type of gift that through the years I have given trees and planted them for special friends, all the while not realizing that this was God's pattern for reminding people of their commitments.

The Trees of the Garden

In the very beginning of the Bible we see the importance that God placed upon a tree. In Genesis 2 we read that God placed Adam and Eve in that phenomenal location known as the garden of Eden. He allowed them to eat from any tree, with the single exception of the Tree of the Knowledge of Good and Evil. Numerous interpretations have been given for this particular tree. I believe it represented God's presence. It was reserved for God alone, for it is God who determines what is good and what is evil. The individual's attempt to eat from that tree indicates a desire to preempt God and to determine what is good and what is evil. In our worst moments, we continually try to "play God" and determine our own set of right and wrong. If we picture good on the right-hand side and evil on the left-hand side, with a demarcation between them, we see that humanity continually tries to move the line to the left—in other words, declaring things that God has called evil to actually be good. That's what happens in Isaiah 5:20, which states that humanity has a tendency to call good things bad and bad things good. Simply stated, this is humanity eating of the Tree of the Knowledge of Good and Evil.

As a consequence, Adam and Eve were ordered out of the garden:

Then the LORD God said, "Behold, the man has become like one of Us, knowing good and evil; and now, he might stretch out his hand, and take also from the tree of life, and eat, and live forever"—therefore the LORD God sent him out from the garden of Eden, to cultivate the ground from which he was taken. So He drove the man out; and at the east of the garden of Eden He stationed the cherubim and the flaming sword which turned every direction to guard the way to the tree of life. (Gen. 3:22-24, NASB)

Now humanity, having chosen sin and having violated the covenant of the garden of Eden, was taken away from the Tree of Life—the tree they most needed. Whenever people "eat of the tree of the knowledge of good and evil," that is, make themselves to be their own god, they lose access to the Tree of Life, that is, they bring death upon themselves. But that's not the end of the story. We've been looking at the very first few pages of the Bible. Let's go all the way to the last page to follow the story in this climax.

In Revelation 22:8-9, 14, 17, John writes,

I, John, am the one who heard and saw these things. And when I had heard and seen them, I fell down to worship at the feet of the angel who had been showing them to me. But he said to me, "Don't do that. I am a fellow servant with you" . . . Blessed are those who wash their robes, that they may have *the right to the tree of life*, and may go through the gates into the city. . . . The Spirit and the bride say, "*Come!*" And let the one who hears say, "*Come!*" Let the one who is thirsty come; and let the one who wishes take the free gift of the water of life. (Emphasis added)

The Impact of Calvary's Tree

Notice the radical change from Genesis. In Genesis a guard was put around the Tree of Life. Adam and Eve were cast out; they had no access to the tree that would provide life for them. But in the closing verses of the last chapter of the entire Bible the tone is precisely the opposite. The angel of the Lord says, "Don't be afraid—you're welcome here." And as if that's not enough, we're informed that we have a *right* to come to the Tree of Life and we can enter through the gates of the city to get to it. We don't have to climb over any walls. And then as if even that's not enough, there's even more. The Spirit says, "Come." And he even says it a second time: "Come." We are *invited* to the Tree of Life.

What's the difference? What happened between the first few pages of Genesis and the final few pages of Revelation? Well, you guessed it. There are two more trees. In the story in which Isaac perhaps carried the wood for the sacrifice up the hill, the Hebrew word for "wood" and "tree" are the same. When the Abrahamic covenant was sealed and confirmed that day, God was essentially saying to Abraham, "Since you have honored this covenant by giving your only son, I can honor this covenant by giving *my* only Son." Jesus carried a "tree" (cross) up on a hill. And he was crucified on that tree—Calvary's "tree"—which made possible the access for all of us back to the Tree of Life, Jesus himself. It's Calvary's tree that caused the tone of the "Get out" in Genesis 3 to be changed to "Come in" in Revelation 22. The planting of a tree is a significant part in the covenant-making ceremony.

Ancient Tribes

Even in primitive tribes of the East, this tree-planting practice was followed. In Burma this has been followed through the centuries. In Timor, Trumbull reports that a fig tree was a witness to the rite of covenant making. It is stated that one missionary had to "cut covenant" over fifty times with different tribes in order to have an effective and safe stay. When he entered into the tree-planting aspect of the covenant, a chieftain informed the people of his tribe that Mr. Stanley was now their "beloved brother."[1] It is believed that the reason the trees at Hebron are so prominent in Scripture is that they were actually witnesses to the covenant being made between Abraham and three Amorite chiefs (Gen. 13:18; 14:13; 18:1).

The Blood-Stained Tree

Not only is it intriguing that primitive cultures establish covenant by tree planting, but it is even more fascinating that some cultures have practiced this rite by a blood-stained "fiery cross" as a part of their tree-planting covenant-making ceremony. This occurred both in the Scottish Highlands in primitive culture, as well as in the southeastern portion of Arabia. It's significant that the tree was soaked with the blood from the throat of a sheep. The bloody branch was then placed into the earth.[2] The potential symbolism of this ancient rite is profound in its comparison to the blood-drenched tree of Calvary that was stained by the blood of the Lamb of God.

14

STONES AND MOUNTAINS: MORE REMINDERS OF THE COVENANT

We are now continuing our examination of the memorials that were designed to remind people of the covenant that had been made. One such reminder is the use of stones. This practice is found in sources outside biblical times. As an example, Arabians would initiate a covenant by making an incision on the hand or the wrist and then allowing the blood to drip onto seven stones. These stones were then a permanent reminder that they had made covenant.[1]

The Stone at Bethel

However, our concern here is not with nonbiblical sources, but with biblical examples of the covenant. One of the earliest references to stones being used as covenant reminders is found in Genesis 28:18-22, which states:

So Jacob rose early in the morning, and took the stone that he had put under his head and set it up as a pillar and poured oil on its top. He called the name of that place Bethel; however, previously the name of the city had been Luz. Then Jacob made a vow, saying, "If God will be with me and will keep me on this journey that I take, and will give me food to eat and garments to wear, and I return to my father's house in safety, then the LORD will be my God. This stone, which I have set up as a pillar, will be God's house, and of all that You give me I will surely give a tenth to You." (NASB)

One of the reasons stones are popular as a covenant reminder is their permanence. They could be counted on to be in place for several generations.

The Witness Stone

Another example of stones being used as a covenant reminder is found in Genesis 31:45-53:

Then Jacob took a stone and set it up as a pillar. Jacob said to his kinsmen, "Gather stones." So they took stones and made a heap, and they ate there by the heap. Now Laban called it Jegar-sa-hadutha ["the heap of witness" in Aramaic—in other words, a reminder or witness to their covenant], but Jacob called it Galeed [which also means "the heap of witness" but in Hebrew]. Laban said, "This heap is a witness between you and me this day." Therefore it was named Galeed. (Vv. 45-48, NASB)

In the next few verses Jacob and Laban admonish each other that this pile of stones is a continual reminder of how they are to treat each other. In true covenant fashion they announce both blessings and curses, stating that neither one is ever to walk by this with intent of doing harm to the other. And they both remind each other that God is a witness and that he will see this. In verse 49 they even refer to this as Mizpah, which means "a watchtower," signifying that God is watching over them. The point is that this pile of stones was to be a visual aid to recalling the implications of covenant making and covenant keeping.

The Intergenerational Reminder

One of the most exhilarating passages on stones being used as a covenant reminder is Joshua 4. The fascinating part of this passage is that the stones were to be a reminder to the next generation.

Remember that covenant is always *multi*generational. The Lord instructed Joshua to pile up twelve stones as a reminder of God's faithfulness as they crossed the Jordan River into the Promised Land. They had waited so long for this moment, but God slowed them down just long enough to leave a permanent mark for the sake of future generations.

"This pile of stones will be a reminder for you," Joshua said to the people. "When our children ask in later years, 'What are these stones here for? Why are they piled up like this?' then we will have an answer for them" (Josh. 4:6-7, author's paraphrase). In verses 21-24 of the same chapter, after they had put the stones in place, Joshua reminded them again,

> When your children ask their fathers in time to come, saying, "What are these stones?" then you shall inform your children, saying, "Israel crossed this Jordan on dry ground." For the LORD your God dried up the waters of the Jordan before you until you had crossed, just as the LORD your God had done to the Red Sea, which He dried up before us until we had crossed; that all the peoples of the earth may know that the hand of the LORD is mighty, so that you may fear the LORD your God forever."

What a thrill it must have been when many of the younger ones who had crossed the Jordan came back in their later years with their children and grandchildren and heard their grandchildren ask, "Grandpa, why are these stones here?" With a smile, they would tell the story of God's faithfulness many years before. This was a reminder of a covenant that God had not only made but also kept. And he kept it for the future generations as well.

The "Stone of Help"

In 1 Samuel 7:5-12 the Israelites used a stone as a reminder of God's covenant love for them. The Philistines were about to attack the Israelites, but God caused a great thunder to confuse them. The result was a resounding victory for Israel once again. Samuel then took a large stone and placed it between Mizpah and Shen, and he named it Ebenezer, which translates "the stone of help." This stone was not so much a reminder of a covenant made but of a covenant kept—on the part of God. He had once again protected them as he had promised.

The Stone of Warning

If a stone is a reminder of the covenant blessings, it can also be a reminder of the curses that can befall one who does not maintain the covenant. In Joshua 24:26-27 we read that Joshua placed a large stone under an oak tree and informed the people, "This stone shall be for a witness against us, for it has heard all the words of the LORD which He spoke to us; thus it shall be for a witness against you, so that you do not deny your God" (v. 27, NASB).

God as Stone

Ironically, God himself is referred to as "the Stone of Israel" in Genesis 49:24 (NASB). And again, in Daniel 2:34-35, he is portrayed as a stone that strikes and crushes all others and literally becomes a great mountain that fills the entire earth. This profound reference to Jesus is repeated again in the New Testament in Matthew 21:44, in which anyone who falls on the stone is broken, or if the stone falls on the person, it simply scatters him or her.

Both the Old and the New Testaments portray Jesus as the stone, but this time as a cornerstone. In Psalm 118:22 and in Matthew 21:42, Jesus is depicted as the Cornerstone, the main stone of the building. He was placed there by the Father after the builders (i.e., the Pharisees) rejected him.

Paul takes the analogy considerably further in Ephesians 2:19-22 when he speaks of God's household. The foundation is what has been preached by the apostles and the prophets. Jesus Christ is the Cornerstone of this building, by which the entire building is "fitted together" (v. 21, NASB) or held intact. It is Jesus, according to verse 22, who brings us together, thus making us "a dwelling of God" (NASB).

Mountains as Covenant Reminders

To this point we've looked only at stones. Let's take a moment to look at the role mountains play in reminding people of the covenant. In Deuteronomy 11:26-29, Moses preached the second of his three sermons that fill the book of Deuteronomy. He described one of the steps of the covenant once again: the pronouncement of blessings and curses. The Hebrews were reminded that if they obeyed the Lord, they would experience blessings. If they violated God's ways, they would bring the curse upon themselves. He told the children of Israel that when they finally entered the Promised Land after waiting so long, he wanted them to have an additional reminder of the blessings and curses so they would choose to walk in obedience and experience the blessings. He identified Mount Gerizim with blessings and Mount Ebal with curses.

He repeated this in his third and final sermon, found in Deuteronomy 27:12-13: "When you cross the Jordan, these shall stand on Mount Gerizim to bless the people [and he lists their names] . . . For the curse, these shall stand on Mount Ebal [and then he lists the names of those who are to be on that mountain]" (NASB).

The children of Israel were finally crossing the Jordan. As they did, God took them through one more step of the covenant-making ceremony, the pronouncement of blessings and curses. He wanted some visual aids, specifically mountains, to be reminders to them of the covenant he had with them. A group of people stood on Mount Gerizim and spoke blessings on the people: "Blessed shall you be if you obey the LORD your God." At the same time a group of people stood on Mount Ebal and reminded the people of the consequences for disobedience: "Cursed shall you be if you violate the way of the Lord."

The Walk Between the Mountains

But Moses never actually got to see this happen. He only *asked* them to do it on two different occasions in two different sermons. It was up to Joshua to live out this unusual exercise in the covenant-making ceremony, and he did precisely that. Joshua 8:33-34 states:

All Israel with their elders and officers and their judges were standing on both sides of the ark before the Levitical priests who carried the ark of the covenant of the LORD, the stranger as well as the native. Half of them stood in front of Mount Gerizim and half of them in front of Mount Ebal, just as Moses the servant of the LORD had given command at first to bless the people of Israel. Then afterward he read all the words of the law, the blessing and the curse, according to all that is written in the book of the law. (NASB)

Precisely how this occurred is not told in the text. Here is the mental picture I have of it, although I admit I may have taken poetic license at this point. As the children of Israel passed into Israel, a group of people shouted down from Mount Gerizim, "Blessed shall you be if you obey the Lord your God!" The children of Israel looked to the south, to their left, to see people yelling down from Mount Gerizim, speaking the blessing. But as soon as they heard those wonderful words, they heard something much less enjoyable. From Mount Ebal, to the north, would come this stark challenge: "Cursed shall you be if you disobey the Lord your God. Cursed shall be you and your children and your cattle and your oxen and your donkeys. Cursed shall you be in everything you set out to do." The startled children of Israel would gaze to their right, up to Mount Ebal, and see the people who were yelling this grave warning.

The Power of a Reminder

A few months later the Israelites were well settled in the Promised Land. On one particular day one of the young men contemplated involving himself in a wicked act. He thought about it for a moment and realized nobody would see him, so he went to the place where he was ready to execute his act of wickedness. Just before his participation in sin, he glanced around one final time to see if anybody was watching. His eyes were arrested—not by another person, however, but by two mountains in the distance. One was Mount Gerizim, the other Mount Ebal. He paused for a moment. He looked at the mountains a little longer, and then he recalled that day, the day they had crossed the Jordan.

He remembered that from Mount Gerizim they had been reminded that obedience always resulted in blessing. He felt a chill on his spine when he remembered what was said from the other mountain, however. From Mount Ebal the people had shouted that if you violated the ways of God, curses would come upon you. He paused a moment longer, realizing he did not want a curse to be upon him. He desired blessings. Under great conviction, he turned from the sin he was about to commit and made his way back home. That's the way I picture it. Thus was the important role of mountains in the making and keeping of a covenant.

Mount Sinai vs. Mount Zion

No more poignant description of the differences between two mountains occurs anywhere in Scripture than what is found in Hebrews 12. Two mountains are contrasted: one is a place of fear; the other is a place of hope:

You have not come to a mountain that can be touched and to a blazing fire, and to darkness and gloom and whirlwind, and to the blast of a trumpet and the sound of words which sound was such that those who heard begged that no further word be spoken to them. For they could not bear the command, "IF EVEN A BEAST TOUCHES THE MOUNTAIN, IT WILL BE STONED." And so terrible was the sight, that Moses said, "I AM FULL OF FEAR and trembling." But you have come to Mount Zion . . . and to Jesus, the mediator of a new covenant, and to the sprinkled blood, which speaks better than the blood of Abel. (Heb. 12:18-22, 24, NASB)

Look at the indescribable difference in these mountains. One is a place of terror (v. 18). It is Mount Sinai, where the Law was given. The Law said that if you did not keep it perfectly, you would suffer the full consequences of your failure. Everyone knew he or she couldn't keep the Law perfectly. Consequently, Mount Sinai was a place of Law, judgment, and destruction.

But you haven't come to that mountain, the writer of Hebrews says. You have come to a completely different one. You have come to Mount Zion (which generally refers to the church), and to the place where righteous persons were made perfect. How were these individuals made perfect? They were made perfect by Jesus, the One who mediated a new covenant. He died for all the covenant breakers so they would not have to die. Consequently, they got to enjoy the benefit of a perfectly kept covenant.

The writer of Hebrews goes on to say it was Jesus' sprinkled blood that they had come to. The very sprinkling of blood is one more step in the covenant-making ceremony.

The Blood "Speaks"

But there's even more. The writer of Hebrews says that this blood "speaks." And what does it say? It speaks "better than the blood of Abel" (12:24, NASB). Remember that Abel was the first person ever murdered. What does it mean that Abel's blood "speaks"? In the ancient world inanimate objects were frequently personified, that is, given human dimensions and personality. In this particular case, it is blood that is portrayed as talking. Jesus' blood talks—and whatever it says is "better" than what is said by the blood of Abel.[2]

That raises an obvious question: what does the blood of Abel say? For that, we go to Genesis 4:10-11: "The voice of your brother's blood is crying to Me from the ground. Now you are cursed from the ground" (NASB). That is what Abel's blood said. It said that Cain, the one who murdered Abel, would die. He was cursed. But the writer of Hebrews tells us that Jesus' blood doesn't say that; rather, we are told that though we deserve to die, we have blessing instead.

This is the kind of mountain (Mount Zion) we have come to. It is the mount of blessing. Mount Sinai had become the mount of curses, but Mount Zion (referring to our relationship with God through the church) is the place of blessings. That's why the writer stressed that Jesus' blood says better things than the blood of Abel does. In other words, Jesus' blood is our place of refuge. It is the place where we find safety; it is the place of mercy.

The Cities of Refuge

One of the most profound depictions of Jesus in the Old Testament is found in Numbers 35:9-34. It is a description of the cities of refuge. If one inadvertently took the life of another, the passage says this person was to run quickly to one of these six cities. If you made it to the city, you were free. You would not have to pay for the death you had inadvertently caused. This was the place of safety.

Jesus is our "city of refuge." He is the place we run to, and, as a result, we enjoy our safety in him. We find mercy.

15

THE COVENANT MEAL:
THE FINAL REMINDER OF THE NEW COVENANT

In my early days as a videographer, I (Rob) was hired to videotape weddings and receptions. Many of my weekends were spent traveling around Dallas to document the special day between bride and groom. As important as the ceremony was in the afternoon, the best and most memorable footage usually unfolded during the receptions.

People were more relaxed and free. There was food, cake, drink, toasts, dancing, traditions, and genuine celebration between two families now joined together in the context of a marriage covenant. I have to admit I even joined in a few of those train dances with my camera rolling. Some wedding receptions were so much fun to experience that they were more enjoyable to document than the local Dallas sporting events that I also covered as a freelance camera operator!

I learned that this wedding banquet was as important an event in which to remember the marriage covenant as the liturgical ceremony had been just hours earlier.

The Marriage Supper of the Lamb

In chapter 10 we mentioned the Marriage Supper of the Lamb (Rev. 19). The word "supper" in the Greek is *deipnon*, which means "a formal meal usually held in the evening." Jesus refers to a wedding banquet in one of his parables in Matthew 22. Here the Greek word for the phrase "wedding banquet" is *gamos*, which means "a festival or feast" that infers a combination of both ceremony and meal.

Believers in the new covenant will one day participate in the ultimate celebration of our union with Christ through the Marriage Supper of the Lamb. The presence of a marriage supper presupposes the presence of a prior wedding ceremony. Since the New Testament calls the church the bride of Christ it stands to reason that we are not yet "wedded" to Christ. This day is highly anticipated as the Spirit and bride both say to the Bridegroom: Come! (Rev. 22:17).

As both a foreshadow of the Marriage Supper of the Lamb and as a reminder of what Jesus did for us on the cross, he instituted what we commonly call the Communion meal. It has other names as well: the Eucharist, the Lord's Supper, and Mass. (Although the verb form of "Eucharist," meaning "to give thanks" in Greek, is found in Scripture accounts of the Communion meal, none of the other terms are; they were coined much later after the resurrection.) As we stated in chapter 3, once the meal was complete, the covenant was then considered in effect and fully activated. We must keep in mind that as we take the Communion elements in our church services, the new covenant is still hanging on the edge of fulfillment. This ceremony is a powerful reminder of our covenant with Christ, but it doesn't mean we have reached its zenith. This will happen in heaven when the bride of Christ is taken away from the earth to consummate her covenant with the Bridegroom.

More than a Private "Spiritual" Faith

The new covenant demands more than an isolated journey with God in Christ Jesus. We are called to celebrate our union with him in our entire being. This includes our physical bodies. This is yet another reason for the covenant elements of bread and fruit of the vine. These components are a fitting match to the makeup of our own bodies: substance (flesh) and liquid (blood). The bread and fruit of the vine is a door between two worlds: the spiritual and the physical. In this meal, our spirit and flesh meet with the Spirit of Christ and the body of Christ. This statement can be difficult to understand. You may be thinking: "Come on! Isn't taking Communion really just silently eating a cracker and drinking a small cup of grape juice while listening to the preacher read from the same familiar passage in 1 Corinthians 11?" Someone with an uninformed understanding of the new covenant would probably be correct with this assessment. But a person with a sound grasp of the revelation of covenant would be aware of the intimacy of taking Communion. Remember the principle of Psalm 25:14, "The secret [of the sweet, satisfying companionship] of the Lord have they who fear (revere and worship) Him, and He will show them His covenant, and reveal to them its [deep, inner] meaning" (AMP).

When a person takes the covenant meal elements, he or she is tapping into the realm of the Spirit because this covenant is not made by human hands. It is truly meant to be a spiritual experience that incorporates an act of the physical body. It is deep calling out to deep (Ps. 42:7).

May God add his blessing to his Word as you read this amazing passage and consider the wonder of the Communion meal!

Remember Me

When Jesus told his disciples to "do this in remembrance of me" (1 Cor. 11:24) at the Last Supper, he was saying something incredibly important that has been lost in translation over the centuries. In fact, today we can put the word "remember" into two very different camps of interpretation. Let's examine them both and discover how important it is to remember the new covenant in the Communion meal.

The first camp of interpretation is the modern twenty-first-century mind-set of the Western culture. Here the word "remember" simply means to reconstruct an event in the past in order to not forget. It is a mental activity that employs the imagination and historical memory. If this is the definition by which we should interpret Jesus' words around the table that evening, then that command is only to be obeyed by those twelve (and later just eleven) men present. If this is the proper interpretation, Paul was inaccurate in teaching the early church to partake in this new covenant meal.

Obviously something doesn't add up.

Now let's examine the second camp of interpretation. It comes from the first-century Middle Eastern culture. "Remember" to these ancient peoples meant an activity of the whole person: spirit, mind, emotion, and body. It is more than just "thinking about" an event. It is re-creating or role-playing the past experience. It is bringing into the present tense something in the past through a symbolic reenacting. Persons remembering something totally identified and participated in all the powers and effects of the original covenant.[1]

Israel was commanded to "remember" the great Exodus from Egypt every year through the Passover meal and the other rituals that accompanied it. They were bringing out of the past the delivering power of God into their daily struggles of the present! It was a faith-builder. It was a lesson-teacher. It was an identity-reminder of who they were in their Sinaitic covenant with God.

So what is Jesus saying in Luke 22:19-20? He's saying to those who would come and follow after him to "reenact this meal again and again. Don't just look back at the cross. Instead, my finished work on the cross will be brought forward to you so you can receive all the effects and promises of the new covenant! Do you need my peace? Remember the covenant. Do you need healing? Remember the covenant. Do you need strength? Remember the covenant! Take its power and apply it to your life today!"

Living Bread

"I am the bread of life," Jesus says in John 6:48. In this passage Jesus is in a discussion with the Pharisees, and, as usual, they are spiritually dull—they just don't get it. "Your fathers ate the manna in the wilderness, and they died," Jesus says. "This is the bread which comes down out of heaven, so that one may eat of it and not die. I am the living bread that came down out of heaven; if anyone eats of this bread, he will live forever; and the bread also which I will give for the life of the world is My flesh" (vv. 49-51, NASB).

Verse 52 tells us how the Pharisees responded: "The Jews began to argue with one another, saying, 'How can this man give us His flesh to eat?'" (NASB). The Pharisees are wondering if Jesus is encouraging them to cannibalism! In reality, he is saying to them, "*I* am your covenant meal. *I* am living bread for you. If you take of *me*, if you absorb *me*, you will have life. Without me, it's over for you. Without me, you're dead. But with me, you live—*really* live!"

This truth is reiterated in 1 Corinthians 11:

When He had given thanks, He broke it [the bread] and said, "This is My body, which is for you; do this in remembrance of Me." In the same way He took the cup also after supper, saying, "This cup is the new covenant in My blood; do this, as often as you drink it, in remembrance of Me." For as often as you eat this bread and drink the cup, you proclaim the Lord's death until He comes. Therefore whoever eats the bread or drinks the cup of the Lord in an unworthy manner, shall be guilty of the body and the blood of the Lord. But a man must examine himself. . . . For he who eats and drinks, eats and drinks judgment to himself if he does not judge the body rightly. (vv. 24-29, NASB)

Before we participate in the covenant meal, we must examine ourselves. We should not participate in covenant or the covenant meal flippantly. Entering into covenant is a serious thing. In fact, verse 30 states that by *not* taking the covenant seriously, some had died. It is not to be taken lightly.

SECTION V
YOUR COVENANT AUTHORITY

16

EXERCISING COVENANT AUTHORITY

How do we take the covenant teaching and apply it to our lives? Understanding the covenant and living in its authority is fundamental to the victorious Christian life. Grasping the significance of the covenant is imperative if the church is to carry on the work of Jesus.

Our Need for Authority

The purpose of the church is to continue what Jesus started. One problem with the church today is that it does many things Jesus doesn't call it to do.

But if we're going to do what Jesus did, we need to understand authority. In Luke 10:19 Jesus said, "Behold, I have given you authority to tread on serpents and scorpions, and over all the power of the enemy, and nothing will injure you." Jesus said this to seventy relatively new Christians. They had been believers for less than three years; yet he sent them out to change the world.

Lessons from a Soldier

Let's hold that story a moment and go to another passage dealing with authority. Matthew 8:5-13 tells us the story of the centurion, a military official responsible for one hundred people:

And when Jesus entered Capernaum, a centurion came to Him, imploring Him, and saying, "Lord, my servant is lying paralyzed at home, fearfully tormented." Jesus said to him, "I will come and heal him." But the centurion said, "Lord, I am not worthy for You to come under my roof, but just say the word, and my servant will be healed. For I also am a man under authority, with soldiers under me; and I say to this one, 'Go!' and he goes, and to another, 'Come!' and he comes, and to my slave, 'Do this!' and he does it." (Vv. 5-9, NASB)

Jesus' surprise is evident: "Now when Jesus heard this, He marveled and said to those who were following, 'Truly I say to you, I have not found such great faith with anyone in Israel'" (v. 10, NASB). Then Jesus says something that seems unrelated to the situation: "I say to you, that many will come from east and west [those are the Gentiles, outside Israel, and outside the covenant at this point], and recline at the table with Abraham, Isaac and Jacob in the kingdom of heaven [that's the Abrahamic covenant and the blessings this covenant brings]. . . . And Jesus said to the centurion, 'Go; it shall be done for you as you have believed.' And the servant was healed that very moment" (vv. 11, 13, NASB).

Faith and Authority

There's a direct relationship between living by faith, authentic "Jesus faith," and understanding authority. The centurion understood this. "You don't need to come all the way to my house," he said. "I'm a military leader; I understand authority. I have men under me. When I say move, they move. Jesus, just speak the word, and it will happen."

"I haven't seen faith like this in all of Israel," Jesus replied. "Not even among the 'covenant children,' who are supposed to understand the covenant." There's a relationship in learning how to live by faith and understanding our authority in Christ. Let's consider those two together.

Tracing Authority

In the beginning, God gave authority to humanity, specifically to Adam. Genesis 1:26 says, "Let us make mankind in our image, in our likeness; so that *they may rule* [some translations say "have dominion"] over the fish in the sea and the birds in the sky, over the livestock and all the wild animals, and over all the creatures that move along the ground" (emphasis added). Having received "authority" or "dominion" means that God has given you rule over something that isn't yours. The same word is used for "steward" or "stewardship." We have responsibility over something that doesn't belong to us.

Most of us drive our own cars. But if we borrow a friend's car, we drive very carefully, because we know it's not ours. While the car is in our possession, we have the authority and the responsibility to take care of it. So it is with the earth. We "steward" it—have authority over it—but it isn't ours.

Psalm 8:4-6 confirms that we have this kind of authority: "What is man that You take thought of him, and the son of man that You care for him? Yet You have made him a little lower than God, and You crown him with glory and majesty! *You make him to rule over the works of Your hands*; You have put all things under his feet" (NASB, emphasis added). As these verses show, God gave significant authority to humanity.

Adam "Fumbled the Ball"

However, this profound authority, given in Genesis 1:26, was lost: Adam surrendered his God-given authority to Satan. Simply put, Adam "fumbled the ball," and Satan picked it up and ran with it. Genesis 3 tells how the serpent approached Eve and planted a seed of doubt: "Did God really say . . . ?" Eve answered: "From the fruit of the tree which is in the middle of the garden, God has said, 'You shall not eat from it or touch it, or you will die.' The serpent said to the woman, 'You surely will not die!'" (vv. 3-4, NASB). Here the serpent boldly challenged God's authority;

the ruse worked. "When the woman saw that the tree was good for food, and that it was a delight to the eyes, and that the tree was desirable to make one wise, she took from its fruit and ate; and she gave also to her husband with her, and he ate" (v. 6, NASB).

Where was Adam in all of this? As a preacher once said, he wasn't out naming bugs and picking berries. He was in the garden too, but he failed to exercise authority over the enemy. Adam could have said, "In the name of Almighty God, who gave me dominion, authority, and rule over the earth, I command you to be gone"—and that would have been the end of it. But he *didn't* exercise his God-given authority, and because of this, we paid a terrible price for his failure.

Exercising Authority

If Adam really had that kind of authority, how should he have exercised it? God modeled the preferred method throughout Genesis. In 1:3, 6, 9, 11, 14, 20, 24, 26, and 29 the scriptures read, "And God said . . ." God didn't just *think* things into existence; he *spoke* them. He looked around the universe and said, "It's dark out here—let there be light." And light was.

Hebrews 11:2 tells us that the worlds were framed by the *word* of God. Likewise, when Christians exercise spiritual authority, we do it by speaking.

Words have authority in the realm of the Spirit. Like seeds, they are planted, and we reap a harvest—good or bad. In Genesis 1:12 we find the "law of Genesis"—"The earth brought forth vegetation, plants yielding seed after their kind, and trees bearing fruit with seed in them, after their kind; and God saw that it was good" (NASB).

I (Jim) grew up on a farm. Not once did we plant wheat and then harvest corn. Not once did we plant cucumbers and then discover that we had grown strawberries. The law of Genesis is this: *Everything produces after its own kind.*

The implications are enormous—especially for people with authority. We exert our authority by speaking it. When a pastor tells the congregation to stand, the people stand. If a teacher, a coach, a boss, or a parent says to do something, those under his or her direction follow (or at least are supposed to). The power of the spoken word points to part of the reason prayer is powerful and important. It helps us to see why soaking our spirits with the words God has spoken—the Bible—is essential for growth, so that we speak his way, his will, and his word. We are people who operate in the authority of the covenant—we should be cautious with what we say and mindful of the power of the spoken word.

From the Physical to the Spiritual

The law of sowing and reaping works just as surely in the *spiritual* domain as it does in the physical domain. Consider Luke 17:5-6, "The apostles said to the Lord, 'Increase our faith!' He replied, 'If you have faith as small as a mustard seed, you can say to this mulberry tree, 'Be uprooted and planted in the sea,' and it will obey you." Is Jesus trying to teach the disciples the fine art of tree uprooting? No. He's giving them a key to his kingdom. In the previous verses, 1-4, Jesus gave some very difficult instruction. Look at verses 3-4: "If your brother or sister sins against you, rebuke them; and if they repent, forgive them. Even if they sin against you seven times in a day and seven times come back to you saying, 'I repent,' you must forgive them." Certainly the disciples recognized how difficult Jesus' instruction was to live out, just as we do. In fact, many Christians struggle with issues of forgiveness every day. "Increase our faith!" the disciples implore in response (v. 5).

Although Jesus proceeded to talk about mustard seeds and mulberry trees, the disciples knew exactly what he meant. He wasn't really concerned with the seeds and trees at all—he was speaking about forgiveness. When someone wrongs us numerous times, we have an option: either we succumb to the roots of bitterness, or we renounce bitterness. Jesus said that in such moments, we don't need *more* faith—we simply need to *exercise the faith we have*. We can speak with covenant authority and say, "In Jesus' name I renounce a spirit of bitterness." Our verbal response has results because we speak with covenant authority. On the other hand, if we hold on to the offense, it becomes "spiritual cancer." But we don't have to do that. By exercising the authority that is ours, even though we have been wronged time and time again, we can refuse to be a recipient of bitterness. We can say, "By the authority of Jesus I refuse to let a spirit of bitterness come into my life. By the power given me by the authority of the covenant, I rebuke a spirit of bitterness. I will live a pleasant life; I choose to walk in peace."

We Have the Spirit of God

Christians can make these kinds of choices and exercise this kind of authority because we are made in God's likeness. Genesis tells us that God said, "Let us make mankind in our image" (1:26). When God made us, he put a "piece" of his Spirit in us. Some argue that we're simply made from dust. While it is true that Genesis 2 states that the Lord formed man from dust, the scripture goes on to declare that "[God] breathed into his nostrils the breath of life, and the man became a living being" (v. 7). We have the breath of God in us!

God created us to be covenant children. And although our bodies are made from dust, our spirits are made from God himself. First Corinthians 2:12 says it this way, "Now we have received, *not* the spirit of the world, but *the Spirit who is from God*, so that we may know the things freely given to us by God" (NASB, emphasis added).

Let's briefly review these principles. God has all authority. He gave authority over the earth to Adam. Satan contested that authority, and Adam dropped the ball. Satan picked up the ball, and in so doing, all humanity was brought under the curse of sin. Romans 6:16-18 says that we were then "slaves" under him. Humanity relinquished its authority, but it would be up to God to set a plan in motion to get it back—and that's exactly what he did.

17

RECLAIMING THE AUTHORITY OF THE COVENANT

How would God reclaim for humanity the authority Adam so foolishly forfeited? God can't simply rip it out of the hands of Satan. Why not? Because he is a God of integrity. He keeps his word. He gave authority to humanity, and humanity could do with it what they wanted. Tragically, they released control to Satan.

Here's one way of understanding the scenario. After my (Jim's) father retired from farming in Kansas, he leased the farm to my cousin. For the sake of illustration, let's suppose my cousin planted wheat where we had always grown corn. If my father had insisted that my cousin return the land to corn, my cousin could have said, "Well, you may own the land, but I have the lease—I can do with this field what I want to."

Similarly, Adam had the "earth lease." The earth belonged to God, of course, but he had given Adam authority over its use. In turn, Adam (humanity) gave the authority over to Satan. Since a man gave it up, only a Man—Jesus—could get it back. Not surprisingly, the provision for this is in the Abrahamic covenant. You'll recall that in God's covenant with Abraham, as in any covenant-making ceremony, the parties exchanged belongings. In the suzerain covenant (in which a king has everything and a peasant has nothing) the king says, "Everything I have belongs to you." The peasant says, "I have nothing to give except myself." In this case, God said, "I want you, Abraham. I want you, and I want your offspring."

God's Plan—the Abrahamic Covenant

The result is that God gained "legal access" (in the jurisprudence of the universe) back into the human race, multigenerations later, by one named Mary, who was in the lineage of Abraham. She conceived as a virgin after being overshadowed by the Holy Spirit, and God put on earth a Man who is sinless. Jesus—fully Man, fully God—will be the One to reclaim or wrench back the authority from Satan.

Mary's "Seed"

Through the lineage of Abraham, God sets in motion his great plan of redemption, of restoration. Our first clue regarding this is found as early as Genesis 3:15, in which God is speaking to the serpent: "I will put enmity between you and the woman, and between your seed and her seed; he shall bruise you on the head, and you shall bruise him on the heel" (NASB). Every other time we see "seed" (offspring) in Scripture, the reference is to "his" seed, that of the male. But this reference, "her" seed, refers to Mary, who will someday give birth to Jesus. "And between your seed" (God is talking to the serpent, or Satan, referring to demonic forces) and her seed there will be great strife. Mary's "seed," of course, is Jesus.[1] "He [Jesus] shall bruise you [Satan] on the head." This means it will be a lethal blow. "And you [Satan] shall bruise him [Jesus] on the heel." You may injure him and think you've driven him to final death on the cross, but you will not prevail. He will conquer the grave. He will rise from the dead.

Mary's Conception—the Spoken Word

God's covenant with Abraham means that everything Abraham has belongs to God—and that includes his offspring. God now reenters the human race through Mary, a descendant of

Abraham. Luke 1:30-38 tells about the conversation between the angel and Mary.

The angel said to her, "Do not be afraid, Mary; for you have found favor with God. And behold, you will conceive in your womb and bear a son, and you shall name Him Jesus. He will be great and will be called the Son of the Most High; and the Lord God will give Him the throne of His father David; and He will reign over the house of Jacob forever, and His kingdom will have no end."

Mary said to the angel, "How can this be, since I am a virgin?"

The angel answered and said to her, "The Holy Spirit will come upon you, and the power of the Most High will over-shadow you; and for that reason the holy Child shall be called the Son of God. And behold, even your relative Elizabeth has also conceived a son in her old age; and she who was called bar-ren is now in her sixth month. For nothing will be impossible with God."

And Mary said, "Behold, the bondslave of the Lord; be it done to me according to your word." And the angel departed from her. (NASB)

Mary could have protested becoming pregnant out of wedlock in a small town, where everyone would notice. But instead of re-sisting these obvious complications about to enter her life, Mary conformed her heart to the word and will of God. "Be it done to me according to your word," she said. And I believe in that very moment Mary conceived. This is the essence of successful prayer.

What kind of faith is this? The same kind of faith Jesus de-scribed in Mark 11:23, "Truly I tell you, if anyone says to this mountain, 'Go, throw yourself into the sea,' and does not doubt in their heart but believes that what they say will happen, it will be done for them." Jesus wasn't into moving *literal* mountains any more than he was into uprooting mulberry trees. In the Jewish idiom, "mountains" meant difficulties, seemingly impossible situ-ations. Mountain-moving faith says, "God, I know it is your plan and your desire for my marriage not to fail. So in the name of Jesus, by the authority of God, because we are covenant partners, I speak to the 'mountain' in my marriage: Marriage, be made whole. Be made well; be made complete."

The Word Became Flesh

John 1:1-3, 14 says, "In the beginning was the Word, and the Word was with God, and the Word was God. He was in the beginning with God. All things came into being through Him, and apart from Him nothing came into being that has come into being. . . . *And the Word became flesh*" (NASB, emphasis added).

Find out what God's will is—his word, His intent—and you cannot do that unless you're *saturated* with his Word. Soak your Spirit with *his* Word, link your tongue up, and speak *his* Word to the circumstances of life. Don't keep announcing the problem— God knows the problem—but instead, speak his Word to the circumstances of life, for you have been given authority.

Again, I believe that Mary experienced the power of the spoken word, conceiving the instant she declared her conformity with God's Word. And what did she do next? She went and announced to Elizabeth, "The Mighty One has done great things for me" (Luke 1:49). She knew this was so because she had received the word—God's word—into her spirit. This text provides a picture of how prayer works. As God's word—God's will—comes to us, we receive it, declare it, and pray it. And then it begins to manifest in the physical, observable domain. That's what occurred in Genesis. God spoke, and the earth was created. Now he "enforces" his will through us—through people who pray in accordance with his will. And situations on earth are changed. Although the phrase "the Word became flesh" in John 1:14 refers exclusively to Jesus, the Word (will) of God is still becoming "flesh" (being evidenced in the physical world of the five senses) when we pray (assuming that we are praying his word—his will).

Zechariah—Not Speaking God's Word

Not everyone responds to the voice of God with the faith of Mary. Earlier in Luke 1 we find another instance of the angel talking, this time in the temple to Zechariah, Mary's cousin by marriage: "Do not be afraid, Zechariah; your prayer has been heard. Your wife Elizabeth will bear you a son, and you are to call him John" (Luke 1:13).

Zechariah asked the angel, "How can I be sure of this? I am an old man and my wife is well along in years" (v. 18). Unlike Mary, he didn't ask how it would happen, which is an issue of curiosity and faith. Instead, he stated the reason that the pregnancy could not or should not occur. The result of his *un*faith is immediate. "And now you will be silent and not able to speak until the day this happens, because you did not believe my words, which will come true at their appointed time."

Can you imagine the angel saying, "If we don't shut your mouth, we'll never get that miracle"?

When Zechariah left the temple, he could not speak to the crowd that was waiting outside. They realized he had seen a vision, for he kept making signs to them but remained unable to speak. People who understand authority are careful about what they say!

Jesus vs. Satan

For seven hundred years the prophets and those who followed them had decreed that One would be born of a virgin. Every time God does something profoundly important on earth, he gets people like you and me to decree it and declare it in conformity with his authority. That's why prayer is important. That's why speaking his word is important.

Mary's obedience set the stage for the continuation of the cosmic struggle for authority. Through her, Jesus came to earth preparing to take authority from Satan. It was as if Jesus and Satan were political candidates, each with his own platform. Jesus describes both "platforms" in John 10:10, "The thief comes only to steal and kill and destroy; I have come that they may have life, and have it to the full." First John 3:8 is Jesus' "purpose statement": "The Son of God appeared for this purpose, to destroy the works of the devil" (NASB).

In his very first sermon Jesus speaks in covenant language as he defines his mission: "THE SPIRIT OF THE LORD IS UPON ME, BECAUSE HE ANOINTED ME TO PREACH THE GOSPEL TO THE POOR," he says in Luke 4:18 (NASB), quoting from Isaiah. "HE HAS SENT ME TO PROCLAIM RELEASE TO THE CAPTIVES, AND RECOVERY OF SIGHT TO THE BLIND, TO SET FREE THOSE WHO ARE OPPRESSED." This is his "agenda."

Jesus' proclamation is the backdrop for the cosmic struggle between Satan and Jesus. In Matthew, Mark, and Luke, we find militaristic language: the kingdom of darkness versus the kingdom of light—two kingdoms, one with a rightful king and another with a challenger to the throne. One will win, and one will lose.

Battlefronts

The battle between Jesus and Satan rages in five arenas:

1. *The hearts of humanity.* When Jesus wins over the hearts of people, we call that *evangelism.*
2. *The physical body.* When Jesus touches the physical body, we call that *healing.*
3. *The emotions.* When Jesus sets us free, we call that *deliverance.*
4. *Weather patterns.* This is not an area we normally regard as a battleground; however, Luke 8:23-25 tells us about a storm that nearly shipwrecked a boat the disciples and Jesus were riding in. The disciples panicked and woke Jesus, who rebuked the storm. We know that whatever Jesus did was in accordance with his Father's will. If he stopped the storm, then God probably hadn't caused it. But why would the enemy try to sink the boat containing Jesus and his closest friends? When the boat landed on the coast, Jesus en-

countered numbers of demons, which he cast into a herd of swine. The enemy, it would seem, didn't want Jesus and the disciples to reach the coast and drive out those demons.

5. *Death.* Satan ushers in death; Jesus overcomes it and ushers in life. John 11 gives a fascinating look at how the Pharisees plotted to kill Jesus. While the Pharisees were scheming, Jesus charged into Bethany, a village on the outskirts of Jerusalem, and raised Lazarus from the dead. The Pharisees just couldn't see that this Man was unstoppable; they didn't seem to understand that he had victory over death—the ultimate victory being the resurrection.

Today the battle of the kingdoms rages on. It's not for physical turf. It's to see who will rule and reign.

Suffering vs. Sickness

As Christians, we're in the fray. Jesus says we're going to suffer for his name's sake. We will be persecuted and reviled, and people will say all manner of evil against us. We are called to participate in "the fellowship of His sufferings" (Phil. 3:10, NASB).

Without doubt, suffering is part of being a Christian, but we must not confuse suffering for Christ with sickness and disease. In Scripture, we never see Jesus saying, "Brother, I know you're sick and I'm really sorry, but my Father did this to teach you a lesson; since I'm in accordance with my Father's will, I cannot heal you." Jesus never responded like that. He was brokenhearted at the impact of sin and the sickness and disease that had been brought upon the earth (see Matt. 9:36). He anguished over what the enemy had done, so he brought healing wherever he went. Was there any sickness in the original garden of Eden? No. Is there any sickness in heaven? No. God does not bring sickness and disease; they are not part of his kingdom. Well, then—who introduced sickness and disease on earth? Satan did. Therefore, sickness is not God's plan. It was—and still is—Satan's.

Then we may naturally ask, "What about godly Christians who are sick? Why aren't they *all* healed if it's God's desire for people to be well?" That is a superb question.[2] It appears that sickness can come from many sources:

1. *Our failure to care for ourselves.* For example, I recently had some surgery. I can't blame it on God or the devil. As much as I hate to admit it, I violated some basic principles of health, and I paid a price for it. Some sickness is brought on us by our own decisions.

2. *Simply living in a fallen world.* I like to refer to sickness from this source as having been indirectly brought by Satan. It was Satan who brought pain, heartache, sickness, and death. That was not God's original dream, of course. The fall of Adam had horrific implications for every component of life—including our health.

3. *Direct action by Satan.* Simply put, some illness is a result of a direct frontal physical attack by the enemy. For example, Jesus says of the crippled woman he healed in Luke 13, "Satan has . . . bound [her] for eighteen long years" (v. 16).

Notice that in the three above-mentioned sources for sickness, I did *not* say that *God* causes sickness. Why not? Because he doesn't. He's a wonderful, loving heavenly Father. He loves his kids. I (Jim) have four children. I don't want any of them to be sick, and if I had the power to lay sickness on them, I certainly wouldn't do it. Why not? Because I love them. If an earthly father loves like this, how much more does our heavenly Father love us? "Every *good* and every *perfect gift* is from above" (James 1:17, emphasis added).

"But wait a minute," you may say. "I know that God ministers profoundly when people are sick." That's true. All of us hear more clearly from God when we have faced difficult physical pain and illness. And God's presence is spectacular in times of suffering caused by a disease. But that still does not mean that *God sent* the disease.

In summary, don't confuse "suffering" with "sickness." Will we suffer for Christ? Yes! The Scriptures repeatedly tell us that we will suffer. In fact, the verse that God used to call me to the pastoral ministry states that "it has been granted for Christ's sake, not only to believe in Him, but also to suffer for His sake" (Phil. 1:29, NASB). However, suffering and sickness are not the same. If we're going to truly identify with the suffering of Jesus, we're going to have to do it some other way than through sickness, because he was never sick. But he did suffer. He went to the cross. And he asks us to do the same.

"Luck" vs. God's Blessing

I (Jim) recently heard of a couple being interviewed on television. "We don't know why *God caused* our child to be born deformed," they said. "But we were *lucky* and found a plastic surgeon to repair the damage" (emphasis added). Their approach would have been more biblical if they had said, "We don't understand why in the course of human events, in this broken world that has been ravaged and traumatized by the enemy, our child was born this way. But, praise God, in his wisdom he released medical knowledge on a group of surgeons. He gave us the ability to gain strength and wealth to be able to afford help, and he brought our paths together. And, thank God—we were able to find help." Do you see the difference? We hang sickness on God. Jesus never viewed it that way. He viewed it as a contested area. He brought health and healing everywhere he walked.

"Fire Truck Syndrome"

Many church people suffer from what I call "fire truck syndrome." I grew up on a farm nine miles from our small town. As a child, I saw a fire truck only two times, and both times I noticed it was beside a house that was burning. I mistakenly assumed that firefighters on fire trucks must start fires, because they were always "at the scene of the crime."

This is what happens in church. Sometimes Satan comes along and beats the living daylights out of somebody, and because God shows up with an amazing force of his presence, people assume that God did the damage.

The truth is that the enemy may bring horrible things, but God can turn them for good. The fire truck was there, but the fire truck didn't start the fire. I once heard of a man who said, "Well, God broke my leg. He knew I needed a rest, so he put me in the hospital for a month." What kind of a God would that be? If I did the same to my son, I'd be in jail for child abuse. If God committed half the atrocities he is accused of, he ought to be arrested! If he wants us to rest, he can put us in a cabin beside a lake. He doesn't need to break our legs to do it.

The enemy traumatizes us and brings wounding, heartache, and trauma. In the midst of that, God's presence comes. Due to God's presence, some people mistakenly assume that God *sent* the calamity. No, he ministers *in spite of* the tragedy, not *because of* it. If we want to know God's will about sickness and pain, let's look at what Jesus did. He's a "chip off the old block." He's the "spitting image of his Dad." Jesus was always in total conformity to his Father's will. And again, Jesus never once said, "I can't heal you, because my Father brought this on you." He brought healing, deliverance, and hope.

God's Work vs. Satan's Work

Acts 10:38 tells us, "You know of Jesus of Nazareth, how God anointed Him with the Holy Spirit and with power, and how He went about doing good and healing all who were *oppressed by the devil*, for God was with Him" (NASB, emphasis added). Notice who is oppressing—the devil. But Jesus came "to destroy the works of the devil" (1 John 3:8, NASB).

Luke 13, which we looked at previously, demonstrates this truth profoundly. When Christ encountered the woman who was bent over and in great pain, he asked, "Who is this daughter of

Abraham that she should be traumatized like this?" Daughter of Abraham? Abraham had been deceased for two thousand years. Why was he referring to Abraham?

Because she was part of the Abrahamic covenant. She was a "covenant child," yet she was in bondage to infirmity because Satan had oppressed her (Luke 13:16). In essence Jesus was saying, "Satan, who do you think you are, messing with one of the covenant kids? You have no right to do that. I put a stop to it!" Jesus came to set the captives free!

18

RULING AND REIGNING IN
ACCORDANCE WITH THE COVENANT

The battle rages throughout the ages—Jesus versus Satan. Although we should not underestimate our enemy, we should not give him too much credit either. Satan is *not* all-knowing. He is *not* omnipotent—all-powerful. He is *not* omnipresent. God alone has those qualities.

Satan's Ignorance

In Scripture it seems that Satan underestimates Jesus, seeming not to understand fully who he is. Jesus is a puzzle to the demonic forces—they understand his *divinity*, but it seems they cannot comprehend his full *humanity*. They accept the fact that he is *God*, but they challenge the fact that he is man. The demons appear to be confused.

In Luke 4 we see a demon crying out through a human being: "What business do we have with each other, Jesus of Nazareth? Have You come to destroy us? I know who You are—*the Holy One of God!*" (v. 34, NASB, emphasis added). This passage is especially interesting because early in his ministry Jesus didn't tell people who he was. Even his best friends didn't know. In fact, he didn't talk openly about his identity until well over halfway through his three-and-one-half-year ministry. But the demons knew, and they blurted out the information. "What are You doing here, God?" they exclaimed. Yet, despite this knowledge they still didn't seem to understand this One who is not the *son of Adam* (under the curse of sin), but the *Seed of Abraham* (totally sinless, thus not under their direction).[1]

The Importance of Jesus' Humanity

Jesus' humanity gave him *legal* standing to be on earth (it was created for humanity) and consequently the right to win back the authority Adam lost. In Matthew 8:28-29, the demons are again confused about his humanity: "When He came to the other side into the country of the Gadarenes, two men who were demon-possessed met Him as they were coming out of the tombs. They were so extremely violent that no one could pass by that way. And they cried out, saying, 'What business do we have with each other, *Son of God?* Have You come here to torment us *before the time?'*" (NASB, emphasis added).

Once again, the demons understood that Jesus was fully the Son of God, but they did *not* seem to understand that he was also fully human, legally (rightfully) occupying earth, and was about to wrench back the authority that humanity—Adam—had surrendered. Though they were aware that at some point they would be destroyed—"Have You come here to torment us *before the time?*"—they taunted Jesus for coming when he did.

In Mark 5:6-7 we see a similar scenario: "Seeing Jesus from a distance, he ran up and bowed down before Him; and shouting with a loud voice, he said, 'What business do we have with each other, Jesus, *Son of the Most High God?* I *implore* You *by God*, do not torment me!'" (NASB, emphasis added). What we have here is a demon shrieking for God's help.

Since when did demons get the idea that they could appeal to God to get Jesus off their backs? But that's precisely what happens in this text. The word "implore" is a military term. Some translations use "adjure." The meaning of what the demon is saying is "I command you. I command you, by the authority of God: stop tormenting me." This demon has the audacity to appeal to God to get Jesus to stop tormenting him. Why? This demon knows he has the right to be here, because Adam handed control over to the devil and his hosts long ago when he sinned. But this demon doesn't grasp who Jesus really is. A man's (Adam's) sin gave them (the demons) power; it would take another Man to get it back. This demon cannot comprehend that Jesus could be fully *man* without ever coming under the control of Satan, that he could be absolutely sinless and that he could resist every temptation. Jesus never thought a wrong thought, spoke a wrong word, or was ever out of conformity with God's will. This One who is fully Man, yet sinless, prevails over the demonic hosts.

Most believers don't understand the nature of Jesus. We can't grasp the fact that he was fully human, that he *had* to be fully human to break the curse of Adam's sin; that to break the curse, Jesus had to be just like us. John 5:26-27 confirms this: "For just as the Father has life in Himself, even so He gave to the Son also to have life in Himself; and He [God the Father] gave Him authority to execute judgment, because He is the Son of *Man*" (NASB, emphasis added). Yes, Jesus is fully God, but for our sakes he is also fully human, yet sinless.

Theories of the Atonement

Jesus wins, and Satan is defeated; it's the story of the cross. So how does the death and resurrection of this God-Man touch our lives today? As we look at the cross, we can study the five or six theories of atonement. We can consider the cross from various vantage points and come away with different understandings of exactly what happened. While most of these theories are probably valid interpretations, we'll consider just one that is especially relevant to covenant. In doing so, we must not overlook the fact that the atonement is essentially about reconciliation. It is about God's loving-kindness—his covenant love—reaching out to restore sinful humanity's broken relationship with him.

Satan on Death Row

In the view of the atonement we will explore, Jesus was pressed to the cross by a murderous scheme of Satan. Just one week before, he had come into town a hero. On Palm Sunday the crowd had laid down branches saying, "Hosanna! Blessed is he who comes in the name of the Lord!" (Mark 11:9). But then a few days later the crowd turned into a murderous mob screaming, "Crucify him!" (15:13). Satan had incited the crowds and ignited the fury of the Roman leaders, so they executed the One who knew no sin. The threat to Satan's reign was over—or so he thought.

When Jesus died, he did not have any personal sin for which he was dying. He was dying as an innocent man—completely spotless, completely sinless. Not once was he out of alignment with the perfect will of the Father, and though he was enormously tempted, he was successful against it and therefore never came under Satan's control. So when he died on the cross, he died spotless, and at that point Satan became a murderer and thus committed himself to "death row." He knew he was defeated. Innocent blood was shed, the provision for sin had been met, and Satan had sealed his own demise.

The impact of Jesus' death is emphasized in Hebrews 2:14, which says, "Since the children share in flesh and blood, He Himself [Jesus] likewise also partook of the same [became a man like us], that through death [Jesus' death] He might render powerless [strip away all the authority of] him who had the power of death, that is, the devil" (NASB).

Colossians 2:14-15 confirms the power of Jesus' death on the cross: "Having canceled out the certificate of debt consisting of decrees against us, which was hostile to us; and He [Jesus] has taken it out of the way, having nailed it to the cross. When He had disarmed [stripped of all authority] the rulers and authorities [Satan and his demonic kingdom], He made a public display of them, having triumphed over them through Him" (NASB). In Christ's death, the provision for Adam's sin and ours had been met. Moreover, through this act of sacrificial love the way was opened for every person to have with God, through faith, a restored, close relationship.

Satan's Presumed Power

If Jesus won at the cross, why does Satan give believers so much trouble today? If he was defeated, why does he seem to have so much power? If you're a student of World War II, you'll remember the gap between D-Day and V-Day. The United States' participation in the European theater of war stretched over a span of approximately four years, from 1941 to 1945. V-Day signified the end of the war, when the Allied Forces, including the United States, were victorious. The enemy surrendered. But about a year before that, there was D-Day. On D-Day it became obvious that the Allied Forces would prevail. Germany had been crushed and would not win the war. Despite the certain defeat, Germany made one last attempt. During that one-year span there were more Allied casualties than in all the rest of the war put together.

Spiritually, we are between D-Day and V-Day. Satan knows he has been defeated, but until we get to V-Day, when the enemy will be finally destroyed, he is staging one last all-out attack.

We're in the interim now, and Satan is wreaking havoc on earth. But how could one who was stripped of his power seem to have so much strength? Here's a way to illustrate the answer to this question: Picture a bank robber who pulls a gun on a security guard in the bank. "Reach for the sky!" the robber says. Who has the *authority* and who has the *power* in this situation? The security guard has the authority, because he wears the badge. But he doesn't have the power—because someone else is holding the gun. But as time passes, the security guard looks closely at the gun and sees that, though it looks real, it's actually a child's toy pistol. At that point he pulls for his own gun. Now who has the power? He who has the authority (the badge) now has the power (the gun). But until the security guard discovered that the robber's pistol was only a toy, he was controlled by fear and deception.

Our Authority and Our Power

Many Christians are like the security guard. We know we have authority over the earth, because God gave it to us. But the enemy comes in with what looks real but isn't (like the toy gun) and rules by fear and deception. Too many times he pulls the gun on us, and we reach for the air, dropping our weapons. In that situation, although we have the authority, we lack the power. We need to realize that Satan's power is counterfeit. Ours is real. We have the authority (legal right) to be here on earth, and we should use the power God has given us.

Ruling and Reigning

Jesus gave authority to the church. Why? According to a well-known confession of faith, the Westminster Shorter Catechism, our chief end (purpose) on earth is "to glorify God and enjoy him forever." Amazingly, the God of the universe desires a relationship with us. He demonstrates the intensity of this desire and his love for us through Christ's sacrifice on the cross. This is, again, at the center of the atonement, but worshipping God and enjoying our renewed relationship with him is not the only reason he gives us authority.

The Climax of History

All of history is heading toward one great culmination, the Marriage Supper of the Lamb, that grand climax of time and eternity in which the church will become the bride of the Lamb, the bride of Christ. When that happens, the bride, according to the Scripture, becomes a co-sovereign, co-eternal ruler with Christ. In the meantime, we have to learn how to rule and reign.

Paul Billheimer's *Destined for the Throne* describes it this way:

1. The earth was created to provide a suitable habitation for the human race.
2. The Messiah came for only one purpose—to give birth to his church.
3. History is headed for one grand climax. The culmination of history is the Marriage Supper of the Lamb.
4. The church will be "the bride, the wife of the Lamb," according to Revelation 21:9. The church will be the eternal companion of Jesus. Ephesians 5:25, 32 says it this way: "Husbands, love your wives, just as Christ loved the church and gave himself up for her. . . . This is a profound mystery—but I am talking about Christ and the church."
5. After the wedding, the bride will be Christ's eternal companion who will sit with him on the throne . . . and will rule and reign with him.
   - First Corinthians 6:2-3 says, "Do you not know that the Lord's people will judge the world? . . . Do you not know that we will judge angels?"
   - Second Timothy 2:12 says, "If we endure, we will also reign with him."
   - In Revelation 2:26 Jesus says, "To the one who is victorious and does my will to the end, I will give authority over the nations."
   - In Revelation 3:21 Jesus says, "To the one who is victorious, I will give the right to sit with me on my throne, just as I was victorious and sat down with my Father on his throne."
   - Revelation 5:10 confirms, "They will reign on the earth."
6. We must be prepared for ruling and reigning. When you "marry into royalty," you have to be prepared for this royal role. God has provided "on-the-job training." It is called prayer.
7. If the church will not pray, God will not act. God will not go "over the head" of his church to enforce his decisions.

8. Through prayer you are an enforcer of heaven's will . . . on earth. You are implementing his decisions here. Through prayer you have been given authority and administrative responsibilities for earthly events.[2]

Notice how often the phrase "on earth" appears in Matthew 16:19 and 18:18-19.

- Matthew 16:19 (emphasis added): "Whatever you bind on *earth*"; "Whatever you loose on *earth*"
- Matthew 18:18-19 (emphasis added): "Whatever you bind on *earth*"; "Whatever you loose on *earth*"; "If two of you on *earth* agree"

Our Power: Prayer

Paul Billheimer wrote, "Heaven holds the key by which decisions governing earthly affairs are made, but we are the key by which these decisions are implemented. . . . Prayer is not overcoming reluctance in God. It is not persuading Him to do something He is unwilling to do. It is implementing His decision."[3]

Many Christians have an inadequate view of prayer. We look toward God, pleading for him to do that which we secretly believe he is unwilling to do. In reality, God wants us to speak that which is in conformity with his Word, his will, and his way. He wants us to bind and loose that which he has already declared to be bound and loosed in heaven. Simply put, *he's on our team (or we're on his)! He's cheering for us!*

This is why we pray, "Your kingdom come, your will be done, on earth as it is in heaven" (Matt. 6:10). It is not effectual to beg God to do things he has already committed to do. We see in Scripture that every time God does something on earth, he gets humans to agree and declare it and decree it—sometimes centuries before it actually takes place. Remember that Isaiah, speaking seven hundred years before Christ, decreed that a baby would be born of a virgin. He spoke in conformity with God's word, and it happened!

Too Busy to Pray

Billheimer has an answer for those of us who protest we are too busy to pray:

Too busy watching television, following sports, hunting, fishing, swimming, boating, engaging in farming or business, moonlighting. We are so busy with the cares and pleasures of this life trying to keep with the trend in new cars, new homes, new appliances, new furniture, etc., that we do not have time to pray. Someone has described a modern American as a person who drives a bank-financed car over a bond-financed highway on credit card gas to open a charge account at a department store so he can fill his Savings and Loan-financed home with installment-purchased furniture. May this not also be a description of many modern professed Christians? And may this not be one reason why modern Christians have so little time to pray?

If you can buy the new car, the new home, the new furniture, the new gadgets, hold down two jobs, and so on for the glory of God, well and good. But if we didn't have to have such a high standard of living, would we not have more time to pray? If we were not so intoxicated with travel, pleasure, vacations, and recreation, would we not have more time to pray? If we were not so enamored of sports and entertainment, would we not have more time to pray? We have more leisure than ever before—but less time to pray. We are not only cheating God and the world, but we are cheating ourselves. By our failure to pray, we are frustrating God's high purpose in the ages. We are robbing the world of God's best plan for it, and we are limiting our rank in eternity.[4]

Seeing What the Father Is Doing

The key to effective prayer, to operating in his kind of power and authority, is to stay tuned-in to the Father. We don't pray for things that are out of conformity with God's will; instead we find out what the Father is doing, and like Jesus, we become one in accord with him.

The key to knowing God's will is to see what he's doing. In John 5:19 Jesus says, "I say to you, the Son can do nothing of Himself, unless it is something He sees the Father doing" (NASB). This idea is repeated four more times in this same Gospel: "I can do nothing on My own initiative" (5:30, NASB); "I do nothing on My own initiative, but I speak these things as the Father taught Me" (8:28, NASB); "For I did not speak on My own initiative" (12:49, NASB); "I do not speak on My own initiative, but the Father abiding in Me does His works" (14:10, NASB). What Jesus is saying in these five verses is, "I don't do what I do on my own. I look and see what the Father is doing. I know his will, his word, his way. I speak it. I act on it." This simple strategy of Jesus is to be *our* "game plan" as well. Let's see what the Father desires to initiate, and then decree (pray) it.

Kingdom, Come!

Every time we pray the Lord's Prayer, we declare, "Kingdom, come! Will of God, be done!"

What is the kingdom we pray for? "Kingdom" here means God's rule and reign. It means Jesus' rule and reign. We aren't supposed to timidly ask, "Kingdom, would you like to come? Will of God, would you like to be done?" No—we are to boldly declare, "Kingdom, come! Will of God, be done!" Where? On earth, just as it is in heaven. Jesus has given us keys to the kingdom, and we have the authority to pray onto earth heaven's will.

When we pray, the kingdom comes, manifested in healing and deliverance, as Matthew 9:35 declares. The same theme is repeated in Matthew 10:7-8 and 12:28. It appears again in Luke 10:9 when Jesus tells the seventy young believers that "if people wonder why they were healed from sickness, just tell them that they got a little too close to the kingdom!" (author's paraphrase).

But the kingdom's manifestations are more than healing and deliverance. When the kingdom comes, there's a flurry of evangelistic fruit as hearts are moved from wickedness toward the cross. When the kingdom comes, hearts are drawn to righteousness, to holiness, to sanctification. When the kingdom comes, there is deep concern for the poor, the downtrodden, and the impoverished (Luke 4:18). When the kingdom comes, there is an outbreak of peace and joy. When the kingdom comes, loving-kindness and reconciliation happens; relationships are restored. Simply put, amazing things happen when the kingdom comes. And that's what we're praying and decreeing when we say, "Kingdom, come!"

A Prayer for Us All

Paul prays for us in Ephesians 1:18-20 to grasp the implications of our covenant relationship. Notice the covenant language:

I pray that the eyes of your heart may be enlightened, so that you may know what is the hope of His calling, what are the riches of the glory of *His* inheritance [the swapping of assets is the inheritance] in the saints, and what is the surpassing greatness of *His* power [the exchange of power and authority and strengths] toward us who believe. These are in accordance with the working of the strength of *His* might [the exchange of strengths] which He brought about in Christ, when He raised Him from the dead, and seated Him at His right hand in the heavenly places. (NASB, emphasis added)

Simply stated, such promises are for all of us and we can look forward to receiving them.

Timing

The covenant promises are not invalidated if they are slow in coming. I agree with the one who said, "God may never be late, but he certainly misses all the good opportunities to be early!" Sometimes a covenant promise comes long after we have prayed it, spoken it, or decreed it. In Joshua 1 we see the Israelites entering into the Promised Land. Let us not forget that the fulfillment of the promise was six hundred years after the promise was made. Long before, the Lord made a covenant with Abram, saying, "I'm giving you the land." For four hundred years the Israelites were slaves in a lonely land. Another two hundred years is not even referenced in this biblical narrative. It was six hundred years between the time the promise was made and the time the people entered the Promised Land, described in Joshua 1.

The fact that there is a long duration does not diminish our confidence in the covenant. The covenant is never invalidated by virtue of taking a long time to fulfill. In the meantime, Christians are to live in power and authority without fear; it is our privilege to rule and reign in the kingdom of God.

The Covenant—Final Thoughts

H. Clay Trumbull, in his turn-of-the-century "earth-shattering" work on the covenant, cited an elderly missionary from Philadelphia by the name of R. M. Luther. Luther had been a missionary among the Karens in Burma. Luther had seen covenant making for many years and made this amazing statement: "I have never heard of the blood covenant being broken. . . . The way in which the blood covenant was spoken of always implied that its rupture was an unheard-of thing."[5]

Let us close this book by saying that we have never heard of the covenant being kept by any human; but on the part of God the Father and on the part of his Son Jesus Christ, we have never heard of the covenant being broken. At its heart, the covenant is an expression of God's faithful, enduring love, demonstrated unsurpassably in the death of Christ, from which flows reconciliation, relationship, authority, and many treasures more. The covenant was not merely made—it was lovingly kept for you and for us, and we enjoy the inexplicable benefits of it.

NOTES

Chapter 1

1. John Hagee, *The Blood Covenant*, God of Covenant Series (Toronto: John Hagee Ministries, n.d.), CD-ROM.

2. Jackson Senyonga, transcript from interview with Rob Price 2005.

3. H. Clay Trumbull, *The Blood Covenant* (1893; reprint, Kirkwood, MO: Imprint Books, 1975), 297.

4. Ibid., 263-64, emphasis added.

Chapter 2

1. Robert E. Coleman, *The New Covenant* (Deerfield, IL: Christian Outreach, 1984), 86.

2. Malcolm Smith, *The Lost Secret of the New Covenant* (Tulsa, OK: Harrison House, 2002), 12-13.

Chapter 3

1. See Duane Weis, *Paid for in Blood* (Dallas: self-published, n.d.), 58.

2. Al Truesdale and Bonnie Perry, *A Dangerous Hope: Encountering the God of Hope* (Kansas City: Beacon Hill Press of Kansas City, 1997), 27.

3. Bob Phillips, *Covenant: Its Blessings—Its Curses* (Lindale, TX: World Challenge, 1986), 9.

4. E. W. Kenyon, *The Blood Covenant* (n.p.: Gospel Publishing Society, 1997), 12.

5. Coleman, *New Covenant*, 86.

6. Malcolm Smith, transcript from interview with Rob Price, 2005.

7. Weis, *Paid for in Blood*, 111-12.

Chapter 4

1. Smith, *Lost Secret*, 12-13.

2. Gerhard Kittel, ed., *Theological Dictionary of the New Testament*, Vol. 1 (Grand Rapids: Eerdmans, 1964), 348.

Chapter 5

1. Malcolm Smith, transcript from interview with Rob Price, 2005.

2. Ibid.

3. http://www.trinityurc.net/articles/vosarticle_lookabove19.htm.

Chapter 6

1. http://www.biblebelievers.org.au/moongod.htm.
2. Malcolm Smith, *Blood Covenant Teaching Series*, 2000.
3. Weis, *Paid for in Blood*, 112. Also see Phillips, *Covenant*, 11.
4. Weis, *Paid for in Blood*, 103.

Chapter 7

1. http://www.meredithkline.com/klines-works/articles-and-essays/the
-correlation-of-the-concepts-canon-and-covenant/.
2. G. E. Mendenhall, *Law and Covenant in Israel and the Ancient Near East* (Pittsburgh: Biblical Colloquium, 1955).

Chapter 10

1. For a much fuller discussion of this profound event, see Andrew Murray, *The Two Covenants* (Fort Washington, PA: Christian Literature Crusade, 1995), chaps. 9—11.
2. This veil split in spite of its massive thickness and size. According to Alfred Edersheim, *The Life and Times of Jesus the Messiah*, Book 5 (McLean, VA: MacDonald Publishing, n.d.), 611, "The veils before the Most Holy Place were 40 cubits (60 feet) long, and 20 cubits (30 feet) wide, of the thickness of the palm of the hand. . . . In the exaggerated language of the time, it needed 300 priests to manipulate each."
3. Marshall McLuhan, *Understanding Media* (New York: McGraw-Hill, 1964).

Chapter 13

1. Kenyon, *Blood Covenant*, 6, 12-13.
2. Trumbull, *Blood Covenant*, 318.

Chapter 14

1. Ibid., 265-66.
2. It speaks mercy. See H. A. Maxwell Whyte, *The Power of the Blood* (New Kensington, PA: Whitaker House, 1973), 31.

Chapter 15

1. Smith, *Lost Secret*, 163.

Chapter 17

1. "Only Jesus is called the seed of a woman," according to M. R. DeHaan, *The Chemistry of the Blood* (Grand Rapids: Zondervan, 1943), 25.
2. For a detailed look at that question, see the extensive outline and eight-tape series "Understanding Healing," by James L. Garlow, available

from Skyline Wesleyan Church of Rancho San Diego, 11330 Hwy. 94, La Mesa, CA 91941. Telephone: 619-660-5000.

Chapter 18

1. See DeHaan, *Chemistry of the Blood*, 25.
2. Adapted from Paul E. Billheimer, *Destined for the Throne* (Fort Washington, PA: Christian Literature Crusade, 1975), 22-23, 25-27, 48-50. Used by permission of Bethany House Publishers, 11400 Hampshire Ave. S., Minneapolis, MN 55438.
3. Ibid., 51-52.
4. Ibid., 52-53.
5. Trumbull, *Blood Covenant*, 314.